PRAISE FOR DANGEROUS CHRISTIAN

Dangerous Christian is a refreshingly authentic perspective on the greatest life ever lived—Jesus Christ. The attractiveness of this perspective comes from the authenticity of the book's author, Shay Robbins. As a man, Shay can use his martial arts to defeat a Division I college athlete twice his size in a matter of seconds, and yet, as a father of four daughters, he is as warm and empathetic as a teddy bear. As a husband, he is adored and praised for his faithfulness. As a camp director, he is the best I've ever seen at taking a staff of collegiate athletes on a spiritual journey, in all my fifty years of running camps. As a writer, he is compelling and fiercely committed to scriptural accuracy. This book and the Savior it well represents will change individual lives, families, churches, nations, and the world! You'll be glad you read it and you'll want to pass it on.
—Joe White, President of Kanakuk Kamps

John Eldredge meets William Wallace! Shay has captured the essence of how to live dangerously and on purpose in pursuit of Jesus. A gifted storyteller who also weaves together insights from heroes of the faith, Shay will both challenge and inspire you. I encourage you to invest both the time and the treasure to read this book.
—Jim Subers, President and CEO, Shelterwood Academy

Shay Robbins will ignite your heart's passion for living out your faith fearlessly in a broken, fear-filled world. This isn't a "how-to" book on becoming a better version of yourself, but rather a better version of the source of all life—Jesus Christ. It's a tremendous game plan for intimacy with God that will lead to greater transformation and spiritual authority in your daily life.
—Greg Tonagel, Head Basketball Coach of two-time National Champions, Indiana Wesleyan Wildcats

For anyone discontent with watered-down Christianity, this book is a must-read! Shay Robbins embodies the message of Dangerous Christianity, or said another way, biblical Christianity. May God use this book to multiply dangerous Christians who settle for nothing less than the abundant life Christ has invited us into!
—David Marvin, Pastor of Young Adults at Watermark Community Church

Dangerous Christian is a passionate plea to dive headfirst into the depths of God's love. You will be challenged by passage after passage of Scripture to know this love and to long for the full, abundant life that Christ offers. The stories and illustrations will make you laugh and cry. They will also paint a clear picture of a good Father's love and the way to walk in that power by dwelling in that love daily.
— Bradley Mooney, Kanakuk Institute

In this book, Shay reminds us how important it is to live fully, passionately, and intimately for and with Christ. Shay provides tender anecdotes, strong scripture lessons, and a clear path to help us overcome our fears and to be big, bold, and dangerous Christians.
— Pattye Moore, Chairman of the Board at Red Robin Gourmet Burgers; Author of Confessions from the Corner Office

Shay Robbins writes just like he speaks — with conviction and passion. Dangerous Christian is a "knife in the teeth, let's take the hill" charge for anyone who truly wants to make a difference for Christ.
— Ted Cunningham, Pastor at Woodland Hills Family Church; Author of Fun Loving You

How does God's great love for you translate into how he wants to use you in his redemptive plan? Dangerous Christian answers that question! This message is simple enough for a brand-new believer, yet complex enough to challenge a mature follower of Christ. Shay is tireless, courageous, and a true champion for Christ. He displays a magnificent ability to see God in the ordinary moments of life and to communicate this sense of wonder. This book will touch your heart and draw you into closer communion with Christ. Dangerous Christian is honest, heartfelt, engaging, and straightforward, without preachiness or browbeating. If you want to live a more courageous life for Christ, you can't afford to not read this book!
— Randy Weeaks, Senior Pastor at Walnut Ridge Baptist Church

What I love about Dangerous Christian is that it is written by a man who first found himself in a jail cell as a prodigal, then was introduced to a loving Father relentless on rescuing him. That journey goes even deeper as a husband and father of five who understands the power of fighting for his own family. I once heard it said that a true Christian man is like King David — both a warrior and a poet — a fierce protector and a relational connector. Shay, in his journey, embodies both. And this book shows us how to be both.
— Joshua Straub, Ph.D. Marriage and Family Strategist, LifeWay

Finally, a book that challenges the heart and mind of the oxymoron "Christian passivity". In Dangerous Christian, Shay calls us to look deeper within at what it means to follow Christ and to wage war with darkness. It is time for the Christian to erase the lines in the sand and be all in representing the God that this earth belongs to. It's time to be a Dangerous Christian not an invisible one.

—Marvin Daniels, Executive Director, The Hope Center in Kansas City

In our culture comfort is an idol. This thought now wages war in the hearts of many Christians in the church today. In this book Shay radically challenges the idol of comfort by authentically sharing his story and the story of many others of how God's relentless love compels us to purposely push back darkness and evil with the light of the gospel of Jesus Christ!

—Aaron K. Anderson, Pastor Vintage Church Durham

Life has a way of wearing us down until we get foggy on the life we were saved from and the life we have the capacity to live. Shay writes with clarity about Jesus giving us life and life to the full. This book clears the air and reminds me that I want to be a Dangerous Christian.

—Luis Cataldo, Senior Leader, International House of Prayer Kansas City

DANGEROUS CHRISTIAN

A BRAVE HEART FOR A BROKEN WORLD

SHAY ROBBINS

WITH
LAURA CAPTARI

ROBBINS FAMILY PUBLISHING

All Scripture quotations, unless otherwise indicated, are taken from the Holy Bible, New International Version®, NIV®. Copyright © 1973, 1978, 1984, 2011 by Biblica, Inc.™ Used by permission of Zondervan. All rights reserved worldwide. www.zondervan.com. The "NIV" and "New International Version" are trademarks registered in the United States Patent and Trademark Office by Biblica, Inc.™
Scripture quotations marked ESV are from the Holy Bible, English Standard Version® (ESV®). Copyright © 2001 by Crossway, a publishing ministry of Good News Publishers. Used by permission. All rights reserved.
Scripture quotations marked NLT are taken from the Holy Bible, New Living Translation. Copyright © 1996, 2004, 2007, 2013 by Tyndale House Foundation. Used by permission of Tyndale House Publishers, Inc., Carol Stream, Illinois 60188. All rights reserved.
Scripture quotations marked NASB are taken from the New American Standard Bible®. Copyright © 1960, 1962, 1963, 1968, 1971, 1972, 1973, 1975, 1977, 1995 by The Lockman Foundation. Used by permission. (www.Lockman.org)
Scripture quotations marked CEB are taken from the Common English Bible®, CEB®. Copyright © 2011 Christian Resources Development Corporation. Used by permission of Christian Resources Development Corporation, P.O. Box 801, 201 Eighth Avenue South, Nashville, TN 37202-0801. All rights reserved.

Editing: Laura Captari
Interior Design: Bill Chlanda
Cover Design: Brandon Butcher
Cover Image: Brandon Butcher

Library of Congress Cataloging-in-Publication Data
Names: Robbins, Shay
Title: Dangerous Christian: brave hearts for a broken world / Shay Robbins, with Laura Captari.
Description: North Charleston: CreateSpace, 2016. Includes bibliographical references.
Identifiers: ISBN-13: 978-1537510842; ISBN-10: 1537510843
Subjects: Religious life, Christianity, Inspirational.

Contact Information:
www.dangerouschristian.com
dangerouschristian@gmail.com

Printed in the United States of America

To my wife and best friend, Ashley—
It's a joy and privilege to live dangerously together.
—Shay

To my nephews, Daniel and Andrew—
You teach me so much about approaching life with fearless wonder.
—Laura

CONTENTS

A Note From the Author 11

DANGEROUS POSTURE
1   The Fight 15
2   The Devastating Power of Humility 27
3   Forgiven and Set Free 41

DANGEROUS PURSUIT
4   The Sword of the Spirit 59
5   Seeking God 71
6   Hearing God 85

DANGEROUS PRAYER
7   The Weapon of Prayer 103
8   Daily Bread 117
9   Standing in the Gap 131

DANGEROUS PASSION
10   Disarming Fear 149
11   Wounds Into Weapons 163
12   Run 175

Acknowledgements 193
About the Author 194
Notes 196

A NOTE FROM THE AUTHOR

The message of this book has the potential to wreck your life. It's an invitation to live dangerously. To seek Jesus passionately and step out in faith like never before. What if we lived like we actually had access to the same power that raised Jesus from the dead? This question has turned my life upside down in the glorious, ongoing destruction of my pride and self-sufficiency.

Wherever you stand with God as you read these words, I pray you won't stay there. Our world has far too many passive churchgoers and powerless religious folk. For many years, I was among them. What we desperately need are dangerous Christians — men and women who press in to Christ, love others radically, and push back spiritual darkness every single day. It all starts with our posture toward God, our pursuit of him, and our re-discovery of the power of prayer.

For years, as I sought God about this book, I sensed him saying, "Wait." Then, in less than a month, 50,000 words flowed out of me like a fountain. The only way I can explain it is the Holy Spirit. I am a leader, communicator, and follower of Jesus, but I am not a writer. My friend Laura Captari is. She has taken my Ozarkian language and turned it into a beautiful read. I pray that God would use my passion and her skill to inspire and transform your spiritual walk.

"Write the vision; make it plain on tablets, so he may run who reads it" (HAB. 2:2, ESV). This is my singular desire in putting these words to paper: that you, brothers and sisters, would run after Jesus like never before. May the Holy Spirit use these pages to stir up a sense of urgency and sacred discontent in you. May the God of the Universe awaken a reckless abandon for his kingdom to come and his will to be done through your life.

If Dangerous Christian sets just one heart ablaze, it will all be worth it. I pray, in the name of Jesus, that one heart is yours.

DANGEROUS

POSTURE

CHAPTER ONE

THE FIGHT

In those early centuries of Christianity, Christians did not go into the world apologizing. They went to slay the powers of darkness and undo the works of the devil, and they lived in holy triumph.
—*John G. Lake*

IT WAS A THIRTY-HOUR DRIVE FROM IOWA STATE to my first grown-up job in Hermosa Beach, California—straight through the desert and blazing hot. Strapped for cash, I decided to make the drive without stopping. But too many college graduation parties had left me physically sick, and the heat only made it worse. My red Jeep Wrangler began to overheat, and I pushed back panic as I pulled off the road to let the engine cool down.

The sun beat down mercilessly, and as far as I could see—wasteland. Like my soul. I was tired of fighting. Fighting to be seen, noticed, accepted, and loved. I was fighting God, stiff-arming any work of the Holy Spirit in my life. Ever been there?

Despite my defiance, Jesus was fighting for me. Fighting to capture my attention. It's as if with every party, every hangover, he was whispering, *Shay, this won't satisfy you. It never will. You can never drink your way to happiness, or find a girl who will satisfy your soul. I am here—I have always been here.*

I just wasn't ready to listen yet…not fully. I resolved to make a fresh start in California—to go back to church and at least investigate a relationship with Jesus. But my heart was still hard. Hard and empty and dry. Pushing aside the desperation in my gut, I turned the ignition and pulled back onto the highway.

YOU CAN NEVER PARTY HARD ENOUGH

Flash back a decade or so—I was a lonely twelve-year-old kid, desperate to fit in. Because of my dad's career in the corporate world, our family moved every few years. New school. New community. New church. Most of the time, I felt like an outsider. Needless to say, I was ecstatic when Carl, who was part of the cool crowd at school, took me under his wing.

"Pssst…my house…this evening…" Carl sidled up next to my locker. "My parents are gone for the night. We're gonna have some fun, man!"

I wasn't exactly sure what *fun* meant, but if Carl wanted me there, I would find a way to make it happen. That night, I was exposed to things I'd only heard of—drinking, girls, weed. This was the "bad stuff" I'd been warned about, but it felt so good to be included. For the first time in my life, I was one of the crew. Carl and his buddies were hardcore. They weren't scared of anybody or anything.

And they had chosen me. No longer was Shay the new kid who felt ostracized and made fun of. Throughout high school, I became a tough guy who could pound beers with the best of 'em, hold his own in a fight, and knew how to work it with the ladies.

Living a double life is exhausting, though. I had to come up with some pretty creative excuses to convince Mom and Dad that I was anywhere but Carl's parties. Somehow, I maintained the semblance of Mr. Nice Guy at church on Sundays, but inside I was running from God as fast as I could. I thought I'd discovered what it meant to be a real man, and I was never looking back.

In college, I finally didn't have to hold back any longer. No accountability, no need to be fake. I cut loose, and soon I was the one whose parties other people hoped to get invited to. Tailgating was a huge deal at my alma mater, Iowa State. Whenever our team—the Cyclones—played, I was there. Early, pre-gamed …and ready to get the party on. My outfit earned me the title of Cyclone Commander—red and yellow size twenty-five clown shoes, tattered camo pants, and a red mask. Bare-chested and with a red cape, I made my presence known. So much so that the local news anchor often stopped by our tailgate to get me on camera.

I was tough, confident, and reckless—both physically and emotionally. I knew how to make people laugh and I really didn't care if I hurt others along the way. This attitude gave me a dangerous sense of freedom that could have easily left me dead and separated from God for eternity. But my life was so fast-paced that I rarely stopped to consider consequences. In fact, I felt like I was above them.

One game day my senior year as we were playing corn toss, one guy started getting on my nerves. He kept bumping up next to me, getting in my space. I gave him a few choice words, and when he still wouldn't knock it off, I threw a punch. In seconds, we were hauling off on each other, and a crowd started to show up.

So did the cops. Before I knew it, my hands were being cuffed behind me. In that moment, all the fun and excitement evaporated. I felt embarrassed, small, and ridiculous. The reality of my foolishness was clamped around my wrists. The campus police put me in the paddy wagon, which happened to be parked right next to the stadium. For the next two hours, I sat there as thousands of people streamed past my open window.

Snickers. Laughter. Pointing fingers. "Look, it's the Cyclone Commander." One of my buddies seemed to find it especially hilarious. He doubled over laughing, making sure to point out my predicament to the fans passing by. *Some friend*, I grimaced. I wanted to put my size twenty-five clown shoe upside his head. But mostly, I was angry at myself. And ashamed.

A WAKE-UP CALL

I spent seventeen hours in jail that day. For the first time in awhile, I didn't have an audience. I wasn't special; I was a criminal. It shook me up—I was used to breaking the rules and somehow evading consequences. But as I stared at the metal bars and felt the chafing iron around my wrists, I couldn't escape the fact that I'd been caught. I didn't sleep a wink, but I did a lot of thinking. A war was raging inside of me—the Lord on one shoulder and the devil on the other.

Here I was just months from graduation…and locked up. A warning. A wake-up call. I tried to shake it off. God was tugging on my heart, pursuing me even though I wanted nothing to do with him.

It's no big deal, Shay. The enemy whispered. *It's hilarious—it's a great story. Another notch in your belt.*

Successfully burying the conviction I felt, I partied my way to graduation. I didn't even bother signing up for housing that final semester. I was out late most nights anyway, and would either crash at a friend's place or go home with someone. My school load was easy—Native American studies, scuba diving, and a few other electives. I already had a sales job lined up in Hermosa Beach, a suburb of Los Angeles.

Life is just about to get good, I thought. No more of these halfway college parties. I'm about to break out into the real world— LA, *meet Shay.*

I don't share this season of my life with you to glorify it by any means. Frankly, I'm ashamed. It's really tough to put it down on paper—even now, fifteen years later. I wish that I could block out from my memory what a jerk I was and the way I used people without a second thought. Betraying friends…and being violent, hurtful, and incredibly selfish.

But when I sat down to write this book, there is one thing I committed to—speaking the truth. Having hard conversations. Saying the things that many Christians shy away from. I share these experiences with you so that you know I'm human. I've failed, big time. I've fallen short in the past, and still do in the present. Yet God has pursued me through all of my foolishness and dumb decisions…and he is pursuing you, too.

STUMBLING TOWARDS JESUS

Despite my best intentions on that desert drive to LA I ended up behind bars my first night in town. This was my second night in jail in just two months. To this day, I only remember bits and pieces of what happened. I blacked out.

What I do know is that I couldn't stop myself. I was used to being in control—living wildly by night and being clean-cut and professional by day. But things were starting to spill over and get sloppy. When I was sober, I had to face the fact that I was a stinking mess—that my life was coming apart at the seams. This reality was too painful, so I did what I'd been doing since the eighth grade and partied harder.

God and I? The only time we talked was when I found myself in jail. When I couldn't distract myself with booze or women or drugs. This time, he had my attention.

Twelve hours ago I was making a fresh start—and here I am, again. My life is out of control! Shame spread itself over me like a dark cloak and my stomach churned. I felt sick inside…and incredibly empty. Glamor, success, and popularity were always just around the bend—at the next party, in the next bed, with the next high.

I wanted to turn back to God, but I wasn't sure if he'd take me. Had I fallen too far from grace? And what would "church" people think? Surely, they'd want nothing to do with me if they knew everything I'd been involved in. I was pretty much at the end of my rope, so I figured I'd try. What could be any worse than my current situation?

The following Sunday, I showed up at Journey of Faith, a church just off the beach. I slunk in a few minutes late and found a seat in the back. It had been years since I darkened the door of a church, and I was half-afraid that people would see through my facade into my soul.

"Him—it's him," I imagined them turning and pointing the finger. "He shouldn't be here. Not after all he's done." While this didn't happen in reality, I was most certainly feeling the weight of conviction. I'd mastered the double-life thing before, so I signed up to help with the youth group. It would give me a cover to keep coming to church while I was trying to figure out all this God stuff. And, I figured, if I was involved in serving, no one would ask the questions I was so afraid of facing.

Enter Shawn Peterson. He was different from most of the guys in my life at the time. He was passionate, sure, but he had this weird peace about him, too. He was settled, thoughtful, and introspective — like he knew who he was and didn't need to prove anything. I liked that.

Shawn led the youth ministry at church, so when I expressed my interest, he invited me to get coffee. I pulled in to Starbucks, my heart beating out of my chest. This was it. He'd ask me questions I couldn't evade, force me to come clean, then tell me the church had no place for someone like me and that I had better never come back.

But that day, a very different story unfolded. Shawn listened and said he wanted to get to know me. He didn't push too hard, but he showed an interest. Most of my buddies were only concerned about shallow things, but Shawn ran deep. I wasn't used to this kind of relationship. Tuesday mornings at Starbucks on Hermosa Avenue became the highlight of my week. I was living with one foot in the party scene and one foot in the church, but I kept showing up.

Shawn invited me over to have dinner with his family and spoke truth into my life, but most importantly, he was safe. I wasn't all that honest with Shawn at the beginning, but as time went on, I began opening up to him more.

I was still in a tailspin with God, but I began to value what I'd formerly defined as weakness. Shawn wasn't macho, but he was consistent and stable, in contrast with my college friends. He really cared, and he didn't need anything from me. It was the first time I felt truly loved in as long as I can remember.

THEY FOUGHT FOR ME

I was changing, slowly but surely — my heart softening to the prompting of the Holy Spirit. At a ministry conference that summer, I responded to the altar call, praying my guts out to God, begging him to take me back.

Silence. Nothing.

The audience began to clear out, and I started to panic. So I tried harder. Maybe I'd forgotten how to pray. No more pounding beers, I was pounding on heaven's door. *Let me in... let me in,* my soul screamed. *You have to take me back. If you don't take me back, I have nothing.*

Again, no blinding light. No handwriting on the wall or shift in my heart.

What the heck? I wanted to yell at God. *I tried to give you everything and nothing happened.* Dejected and desperate, I left as the staff were turning the lights out and ran into my buddy Kevin outside. Kevin listened to my sob story about how God didn't want me and must be angry with me, and his response took me by surprise.

"You need to come clean, Shay." Kevin didn't pull any punches. He knew I was living a double life. He'd been caught up in the party scene himself. "I think that's what God is after — He wants your heart, man. You can't pick and choose what to bring to him and what to hide."

Ouch. I wanted to tell Kevin off, but I knew he was right. The Holy Spirit brought to mind a verse Shawn and I had been talking about recently: "Confess your sins to each other and pray for each other so that you may be healed" (JAS. 5:16). I called Shawn and asked him to meet with me and the other youth leaders. I was scared to death. I was sickened by myself — wouldn't they be, too?

Overwhelmed with shame and self-hatred, I blurted it all out. Part of me wanted to get up and run out the door, but I was tired. I'd been running from God for a decade, and I was worn out from fighting him.

All these years, I had thought I was a real man, but little did I realize my honesty that night was the first truly strong thing I'd done in a long time. I told the guys everything — from the drinking to sleeping around to ending up in jail.

And then I held my breath and waited. Waited for the condemnation, the judgment, the consequences that would inevitably come once they found out I was the last thing from the Mr. Nice Guy I had tried so hard to portray.

I was so shocked by their response. Instead of being disgusted, these guys responded with love and care. They saw me — the vileness of my sin — and they didn't turn away. It was dumbfounding, disorienting. I felt a physical weight fall off my shoulders. And in that moment, I began to grasp the forgiveness of God like never before.

I broke down weeping—the messy kind of sobs that wrack your body and leave snot dripping from your nose. I don't remember all that was said that night, but one thing I know: there was grace—grace even for me.

"We love you, Shay…and we're not going to let you walk back into this life." Shawn's words were strangely reassuring. A year before, I would have bucked up against him like crazy for saying that. But I knew I was in over my head. I had no fight left in me to resist God.

This encounter changed everything. I was free—transformed by the Holy Spirit. More than just a fresh start, I was a new man. I was no longer fighting myself, fighting God, or fighting for attention from others. I was still tempted like crazy, but these guys fought with me. They stood in the gap when I was weak and in essence told the devil, "No more. You will not take Shay back." This kind of spiritual toughness and accountability was new to me—it flew in the face of my understanding of Christianity. Shawn said hard things to me—a lot—things I didn't want to hear. But I knew they were true, and I knew he cared.

That night, I began discovering the true fight God created me for. My journey with God has been long and wayward. **But I finally realized what I didn't as a kid—following Jesus isn't for wimps.** It's the most dangerous thing you and I can ever do. Sure, a different kind of dangerous than running from the law or evading jail, but one that is infinitely more satisfying than the temporary high I used to live for.

It's takes toughness and grit to follow Christ. It takes passion and aggressiveness, risk and gutsiness. Living dangerously for the gospel may not look like William Wallace charging across the Scottish Highlands, but it is just as real of a fight.

THE FATHER BY OUR SIDE

My wife Ashley and I have five precious children under the age of seven—Lulu, Belle, Knox, Tess, and Piper, who you'll meet throughout these pages. Having five kids is intense. Intensely beautiful. Intensely exciting. And intensely exhausting!

Every morning I manage to steal a few precious moments of solitude and prayer. I roll out of bed before dawn and meticulously tiptoe my way across our bedroom. One creak of the floorboards and my little rascals will wake up and tumble out of bed, eager to start the day. It's just seventeen feet from my side of the bed to our master bedroom closet, and when I make it inside, I close the door with the exultant feeling of a mission accomplished.

I treasure this time with the Lord. It's often interrupted by the joys of parenting, but this daily dose of solitude and prayer is the most important part of my morning. Recently, I was lying on the floor in the closet when one such interruption happened. I heard the pitter-patter of little feet, and the door cracked open to the mischievous grin of my three-year-old son, Knox.

With his deep dimples, Knox's grin is contagious. I smiled back as he snuggled into the closet next to me. "Hey buddy, what are you doing?"

"What are you doing?" he countered.

"Well, I'm praying for our family. Do you want to pray with me?"

"Yeah."

We bowed our heads together. "God," I said, "Please help Knox and I become the protectors of our family." Protection is a big theme in our household right now. With all his boyish energy, Knox can be prone to inflict injustice rather than stand up against it.

After we said "amen," Knox looked up at me seriously. "Dad, when I grow up, will you fight the bad guys with me?"

I just about burst with pride. "Sure, buddy, I'd love to fight the bad guys with you."

"Thanks," he replied simply, as if expecting nothing less.

That conversation with Knox has stuck with me. There's something deep in him—in all of us—that wants to protect what's good and right in this world. But there's something more.

Knox wants to fight against evil with his father by his side.

What does God desire for us as his children? Does he just want to protect us and keep us safe—to give us a comfortable life until he calls us home to heaven? Or did he create us for more?

"Blessed be the LORD, my rock, who trains my hands for war, and my fingers for battle," the Psalmist writes (PS. 144:1, ESV). War …battle…fight…these are things my wife Ashley and I are usually trying to *stop* in our household.

Growing up, I equated following Jesus with being Mr. Nice Guy. After all, our world is pretty violent. Just turn on the news—bullying, domestic violence, school shootings, and terrorism. The list goes on. In contrast, Christians should be kind, loving, moral, and even-tempered…right? That's the message I got, anyway. *Be a good guy. Keep your cool. And whatever you do, don't get too passionate—that's a fast track to sin.*

Fighting, for all intents and purposes, has become what the "bad guys" do. **But I wonder if fighting itself isn't the problem—maybe it's what we're fighting *for*.**

Despite his imperfections, Knox has one thing going for him. He's passionate. He will take a stand against evil any day, brandishing his toy sword bravely against real or imagined foes. He's got courage. He's got guts. He's ready to fight.

If we're honest, I'm not sure we can always say that of ourselves. Some of us tend to play it safe. We hide. We try to fit in—to be that "nice" guy or girl the church has trained us to be. No fighting on our horizon!

Others of us get sidetracked fighting over meaningless stuff. We cut other people down to prove our point. We do whatever it takes to get ahead. We puff up our chest and strut around hoping to get an "atta-boy" or "atta-girl"—clown shoes or no clown shoes!

Many times, we fail to even recognize the invisible enemy at war against our souls, and how both of these extremes numb us to God.

Could it be that we've settled for a cheap imitation of what it means to know and follow Christ? I know I did—for most of my life.

This book is not about working harder or doing more. It's an invitation to a deeper relationship with Jesus Christ, which can transform us from passive believers to dangerous weapons for the gospel. Only when we fully grasp and experience the love of God can we live dangerously.

Dangerous Christians see the world, themselves, and other

people differently. Appearances don't matter so much anymore. Physical prowess is no longer how we measure strength. Faith is.

Toughness, grit, and passion to follow Jesus—that's what has power to change our world, make the devil tremble, and bring God glory. It's a fight we're in together, joining with men and women across the world and across history. Just like Knox asked me to fight with him, you and I were created to fight against evil with our Heavenly Father by our side.

How can we experience intimacy with God that transforms our hearts from passive believers to passionate warriors? How can we move from harmless belief to wreaking havoc against our spiritual enemy?

It all starts with the devastating power of humility.

CHAPTER TWO

THE DEVASTATING POWER
OF HUMILITY

Humility is the gateway into the grace and favor of God.
—Harold J. Warner

JOE HAS CEREBRAL PALSY. He is paralyzed from the chest down and confined to a wheelchair.

Joe struggles to get his words out through a stutter. But boy, Joe can pray!

Joe's father, Dr. Bob Schuchardt, volunteers as a doctor at Kanakuk Kamps, the sports camp where I am a director. I had heard Joe pray for the first time when he was eleven years old at a father-son retreat. His bold and broken words were one of the most amazing things I have ever experienced in my life. So when we launched a camp-wide prayer week at Kanakuk a few summers ago, I asked Joe if he would come and pray with us.

I pushed Joe's wheelchair down the gravel path toward our weight room, built on the shore of Table Rock Lake in the Ozarks. Fifty of the greatest Christian athletes I know, hand-picked from colleges and universities all across the country, were crowded into that tight space. As I brought Joe into the weight room, the sea of athletes parted and I parked him in their towering midst. It struck me as ironic—so much physical strength and prowess all in one place—and Joe's crippled little body.

The guys took a knee around us, coming down to Joe's level, and I introduced him. "Hey, fellas, this is my friend Joe. He is going to pray for us today."

Without missing a beat, Joe began to encourage them. He struggled to get the words out of his mouth, but he didn't stop. I watched as the guys began to fidget awkwardly. Remember, I had seen Joe pray before. I grinned and thought about how perfect this was. Joe was getting ready to put the ball up on the tee and hit this thing out of the park.

Joe put his mangled fingers together and said, "Let's pray," bowing his head.

The guys put their knees to the ground and their faces to the floor. The first two sentences that came out of Joe's mouth he screamed at the top of his lungs: "I rebuke Satan in Jesus' name! There is no room for the enemy in this place!"

You would have thought we'd all been struck by lightning. Every hair on our bodies stood on end. When Joe prays, he prays with power. I believe it's nothing short of a gift. And when that power comes boiling up out of him, it abolishes his stutter and Joe prays with fervor, passion, and authority.

Joe continued crying out to God for twenty minutes. I could hear the young men around me begin to weep, and I, too, crumbled emotionally — overwhelmed by the power of the Holy Spirit in the room. In that moment, I was keenly aware of God's greatness and love and my desperate need for him. When Joe finally said "amen," I'll never forget what I saw — our tears had anointed the weight room floor.

In the physical realm, these guys were muscled, athletic, and gifted. And Joe sat there in his wheelchair, a broken-bodied little boy. But in the spiritual realm? *We* were the little boys, unable to walk and hopelessly weak and twisted. The reality of our spiritual condition overwhelmed this group of athletes and a wave of humility brought us crashing to the floor.

And there stood Joe, thirty feet tall, with legs like tree trunks firmly rooted in the truth. He held a sword engulfed in flames and at the sound of his voice, the enemy shrieked away into the darkness.

That's a dangerous Christian if I've ever met one.

SEEING REALITY, ENGAGING THE BATTLE

As a young man, I was strong, confident, accomplished—and proud of it. Weeping on the floor was the last thing I could ever imagine. Every time I walked into a room, I was sizing people up. The way I dressed, the way I talked, who I hung out with—it all revolved around trying to fit in, be cool, and get affirmation from others.

Maybe you can relate.

Look out for yourself. Dress to impress. Do whatever is necessary to get ahead—that's how the world works, right?

This attitude is prevalent in our world today. Our 4G, drive-through, instant gratification culture can breed entitlement and arrogance. We're continually bombarded with advertising trying to convince us that we deserve better, more—*anything but* what we have. It's the same mindset Adam and Eve bought into at the very beginning of time.

Created in God's image, Adam and Eve were made to reflect his goodness, strength, tenderness, and creativity. Their calling? To live in intimate fellowship with God and each other—an environment of complete trust, perfect love, and unhindered delight. Out of this life-source, they were entrusted with taking care of the world that God had created.

Can you imagine? God gave Adam and Eve responsibility and ownership for all of creation. This was no small task!

Yet Satan whispered, "Did God really say…?" (GEN. 3:1). With these four words, pride took root. *What about you—don't you matter? Look out for yourself! Can you really trust a God who tells you 'no'? What are you, his slave? You don't need him. You're a big deal. Do it your way.*

It sounded so good, so appealing. To strike out on their own. To be the master of their own ship. But the results were deadly. This Genesis story isn't ultimately about sneaking fruit behind God's back…it's about pride. Pushing God out and trying to do life solo.

Inevitably, pride always destroys intimacy and connection. Rather than fighting temptation, Adam and Eve took up a case against God, and you and I were born into a cosmic battle. "Things are not what they seem," John Eldredge writes. "This is a world at war, and you have a crucial role to play. A battle is raging. And it is a battle for your heart."[1]

Do you ever have a sense that there is more going on than you can see? Make no mistake about it — we're at war. With ourselves. With spiritual forces that seek to destroy us. With the prince of evil himself. Scripture reminds us, "[O]ur struggle is not against flesh and blood, but against the rulers, against the powers, against the world forces of this darkness, against the spiritual forces of wickedness in the heavenly places" (EPH. 6:12).

Reality check. There is a grueling and vicious battle raging just beyond the curtain of our senses. A battle that has high stakes — eternity. Living in this physical world, it's easy to lose perspective. It's easy to get caught up hanging out with friends, getting through school, building our career, parenting our kids, paying the bills, doing ministry — Satan will use anything to distract us, even good things.

As adults, we may not squabble over toys like my kids sometimes do. We're a bit more sophisticated. We fight to be recognized, noticed, chosen, and accepted. We fight over job promotions, ministry positions, and social status. We fight anyone and anything that gets in the way of what we want — if not with our hands, then certainly with our words. We fight for anything and everything except, perhaps, the only thing that really matters.

Satan does everything in his power to distract us from this reality, whispering in our ears the same lies that duped Adam and Eve. Too often, we buy in without thinking. We drink the Kool-Aid of pride, and then wonder why God feels so distant. In the words of C.S. LEWIS,

> We are half-hearted creatures, fooling about with drink and sex and ambition when infinite joy is offered us, like an ignorant child who wants to go on making mud pies in a slum because he cannot imagine what is meant by the offer of a holiday at the sea. We are far too easily pleased.[2]

Getting comfortable on earth means we long less for heaven — it's a dangerous compromise. Pride makes us think life is all about us — getting what *we* want, having *our* needs met, making a name for *ourselves*. So often, we live disconnected from our life source, trying to create our own meaning and happiness. But it never quite seems to satisfy. Striving, success, and popularity leave us empty and in bondage—in a jail cell of our own making. Satan looks on with glee, wreaking havoc in our hearts and in our world.

Sometimes, truth comes to us in the most unexpected of ways, like through a boy with cerebral palsy. You see, Joe grasps what we often forget: "The Son of God appeared for this purpose, to destroy the works of the devil" (1 JN. 3:8, NASB). In the biggest battle of all time, Jesus Christ, the Son of God, broke Satan's grip on our souls through his death on the cross and resurrection. The Greek word here for "destroy"—luó—literally means "I loose, I untie, I release, I destroy."[3]

This isn't just a theological concept—it's a tangible reality of what God has done for us that has the power to change everything. Jesus's mission is "to proclaim freedom for the captives and release from darkness for the prisoners" (IS. 61:1). Apart from Christ, you and I are those prisoners. Just as I couldn't squirm my way out of the handcuffs that locked me up in jail—and Adam and Eve couldn't work their way back to God—we can't shake off pride and commit to trying harder in our own strength to earn God's love and acceptance. Pride is built into our DNA because of the Fall. In a thousand little ways, we push God out of our lives every single day.

We like to see ourselves as tough, independent, and invincible, but in reality, we're handicapped. Our souls—if not our bodies—are broken, marred by sin. We need to be rescued from ourselves. We need Jesus, not just to help patch up the messy parts of our lives, but to break the shackles of pride and shatter the lies that keep us in bondage.

God's Word admonishes us to "be strong in the Lord and in his mighty power" (EPH. 6:10). But what does this look like, practically? Is it brandishing our Bibles like swords and throwing jabs at invisible enemies? Is it pulling together all the grit we can muster to show Satan who's boss?

The word for "strong" here is endunamoó in Greek. It's an action verb that means "to empower, enable, and increase in strength."[4]

In essence, God is saying, "I will fill you with power; I will strengthen you; I will make you strong—not with your own toughness, but with my supernatural power in you."

We need brave hearts to engage with this broken world, and such bravery is not of our own making.

THE FREEDOM OUR HEARTS LONG FOR

My kids love superheroes, Superman in particular. We've had one or two incidents where Knox mistakenly thought he could fly, but soon realized that even he is not exempt from gravity. You and I can buy into a similar myth in our approach to faith. We strap on Christianity like a jet pack to get us where we want to go. But following Jesus is not a self-help project. It's a complete inner transformation that starts with humility.

"If you want God's grace," Tim Keller writes, "All you need is need, all you need is nothing. But that kind of spiritual humility is hard to muster. We come to God saying, 'Look at all I've done' or maybe 'Look at all I've suffered.' "[5] We point with pride to our trophies, our degrees, our bank accounts, our ministries, and our successes, while stuffing away our failures, mistakes, and inadequacies.

But could it be that the things we cling to so tightly actually stand in the way of experiencing God and being used by him? **Perhaps the failures we try to forget—the deep secrets we are most ashamed of—actually hold the key to the freedom our hearts long for.**

In hide and seek, God always wins. That's what Adam and Eve soon discovered. After disobeying God, they were overwhelmed with shame and tried to hide. What God did next astounds me. He didn't strike them dead, or pull out the divine paddle to give them a spanking they'd never forget. No, he sought them out, just like the Good Shepherd in Jesus' parable, who left ninety-nine sheep in search of the one who wandered off for greener pastures (MATT. 18:12).

Have you been following Jesus for years, but find your relationship with him stale and *empty*? You're left wondering, *is this all there is?*

Or maybe Christianity has left a bad taste in your mouth. You've encountered one too many "church people" who are legalistic and hypocritical, and you've given up on faith altogether.

Whatever your story as you read these pages, humility has the potential to unlock the grace and power of Jesus Christ in your life. Right now, today, God is pursuing you. He's not impressed by your accomplishments or turned off by your failures. You can't out-sin his grace and mercy, no matter what you've done. There is nothing you can do to make him love you more. There is nothing you can do to make him love you less.

Just ask King David. This guy screwed up, big-time. He committed adultery with his friend's wife, and then killed his buddy to cover it up. "When I kept silent," David reflects, "my bones wasted away…my strength was sapped as in the heat of summer" (PS. 32:3-4). Hiding our sin never ends well—it will sap us of energy, joy, and life.

But David discovered a better way: "Then I acknowledged my sin to you and did not cover up my iniquity. I said, 'I will confess my transgressions to the Lord.' And you forgave the guilt of my sin" (PS. 32:5). Maybe you, like David, have fallen prey to sexual sin. Or perhaps the failures in your life are more "socially acceptable." I've been guilty of both.

However you've fallen short, one thing is certain: Jesus sees you—the real you, with all of your sins, mistakes and failures—and he longs to set you free. He's aching to. Are you stiff-arming him, trying to pull yourself up by your own bootstraps? I did, for years. When I finally surrendered to Jesus, I realized I had been fighting the only one who could really satisfy my soul—the one who was fighting for me all along.

"God opposes the proud, but gives grace to the humble," the Bible tells us. "Submit yourselves, then, to God. Resist the devil, and he will flee from you. Come near to God and he will come near to you. Wash your hands, you sinners, and purify your hearts, you double-minded. Grieve, mourn and wail…Humble yourselves before the Lord, and he will lift you up" (JAS. 4:6-10).

Herein lies a truth that I fear too many of us have passed over in our attempts to do great works for God: **intimacy with God cannot coexist with pride. It's impossible.** Pride isolates us from the life-giving realities of grace, love, forgiveness, and community. Pride puts us at odds with God and shuts down the work of the Holy Spirit. And pride comes in many forms, often wrapped in religiosity and legalism.

What would it look like to adopt a different stance before God—to abandon our Superman pose and get brutally honest with God?

COME AS YOU ARE

If you want to build a house, you've got to start with a blueprint. You'll also need a good supply of raw materials—cement, brick, joists, nails, shingles, and the like. As God goes to work to develop us into dangerous Christians, he brings all the supplies that are needed.

Except for one thing.

"My sacrifice, O God, is a broken spirit," King David cries out. "A broken and contrite heart, you, God, will not despise" (PS. 51:17). All God asks is that we come to him as we are. This is the essence of humility. Our nature is to hide, pretend, and minimize our brokenness, but the love of Jesus empowers us to come clean with all our imperfections, because "we know and rely on the love God has for us" (1 JN. 4:16). We know that God is working all things for our good, redeeming our darkest secrets and greatest failures for his glory.

Humility is a daily spiritual practice, not a one-time prayer or an item to check off a list. It's an ongoing fight in our world of selfies and self-absorption, iPhones and I-focus. It's the choice to die to ourselves—our desire to prove our point, to be noticed and validated by others.

When we cling tightly to our need to be "right" and have life figured out, we squelch the work of the Holy Spirit in our lives. But when we admit our need and dependence on God, we open our lives to his life-transforming power. The love of God has the power to obliterate the strongholds of Satan in our lives, leaving our enemy with no choice but to flee. That's what made Joe so spiritually powerful. Not a charismatic presence or a bold personality, but a humble heart through which the Holy Spirit flowed powerfully.

If humility is the foundation to a passionate spiritual life, how do we develop it? Since that day I first took the risk to be vulnerable with Shawn and Kevin, I've learned that humility is often born in community. Daily, I find myself wrestling with the pride monster. That's why it's so crucial to surround ourselves with men and women who will keep us grounded in the reality of the gospel. We need safe spaces to confess our sins and bring our failures into the light of God's grace. I'm so thankful for my wife, Ashley, who reminds me that I'm imperfect, fallible—and loved. My co-workers here at Kanakuk Kamps help me remember that I'm not "all that" by calling me out on sin and embodying the grace of Jesus in my life.

Who in your life embodies grace and encourages you toward humility? Are there any steps God might be calling you to take to move into community with other believers?

The more we grasp that we are chosen, delighted in, and precious as children of God, the more pride loses its grip on our hearts and humility begins to flourish. Surrendered to the love of Christ, we become instruments of his good destruction—destruction of selfishness, entitlement, and arrogance. When our hearts are soft and moldable, God can teach, shape, influence, build, empower, and grow us like never before, working through us powerfully to change our world.

It starts as we grapple afresh with all that God is.

THE POWER OF ONE BILLION TRILLION

John Wesley is one of my heroes. This guy was hardcore. An English pastor and theologian in the 1700s, he preached multiple times a day and people flocked from everywhere to hear his message.[6] John Wesley wasn't focused on PR or platform building. Reportedly, he slept six hours a night, waking up at four in the morning to spend time with the Lord, much like Martin Luther, who once said, "I have so much to do today that I'm going to need to spend three hours in prayer in order to be able to get it all done."[7]

What drove these men to seek God with such passion? They knew their desperate need for him. There is no one "formula" for humility — you could get up at four every morning, and do so out of pride and legalism. Humility, then, is not about engaging in certain religious behaviors. It is an attitude of our hearts that flows from an honest recognition of who God is and our dependence on him for every single breath.

"[H]e sustains everything by the mighty power of his command," Scripture reminds us. "For in him we live and move and have our being" (HEB. 1:3, NLT; ACTS 17:28). This is the God that Wesley and Luther caught a vision of. They grasped the reality that without God, they could do nothing — that they desperately needed his strength and grace for each day.

What about you and I? Perhaps our fundamental problem when it comes to humility is that our view of God is too small. Consider, for a moment, the grandeur of the universe. Astronomers estimate that there are more than 170 billion galaxies — and that our own galaxy, the Milky Way, contains at least 400 billion stars. That means, in our known world, there are about 1,000,000,000,000, 000,000,000,000 (that's a septillion) stars...not to mention what is beyond our ability to detect with current scientific technology![8]

Then think about the minute detail of every human cell. All of the DNA that makes you who you are — each chromosome working in harmony with the 37,200,000,000,000 (37.2 trillion) cells that make up your body.[9] If you buy into creation requiring a Creator, it begs the question. How powerful must this Creator be? It's staggering to think of how massive creation is, and yet how detailed every single microscopic element is.

Stop for a minute. Let it blow your mind. God's power and grandeur is beyond our comprehension. Yet this all-powerful God chose to put his humility on display in Christ, "Who, being in very nature God, did not consider equality with God something to be used to his own advantage; rather, he made himself nothing by taking the very nature of a servant, being made in human likeness.

And being found in appearance as a man, he humbled himself by becoming obedient to death — even death on a cross!" (PHIL. 2:6-8)

If Jesus' life is any indication, humility may well be one of the most powerful forces in the universe, for with it, Jesus bought our redemption and salvation. Satan knows well the kingdom power of a surrendered life. Perhaps that's why he works so hard to keep us entangled in sin, distraction, and "good" pursuits. Everything in my flesh wants to buck up against humility. I want to be strong, put-together, and competent. But this is not the way of Jesus. Following Jesus means following him in humility, obedience, and death to our selfishness.

Humility is the bridge to intimacy with God, a relationship that transforms us from the inside out, makes us spiritually dangerous, and sets us on fire to change our world. But to be filled with his Spirit, we must be emptied of ourselves. We must begin to see the world through his eyes, not our own.

AN INVITATION TO LIVE DANGEROUSLY

A few weeks after I made the decision to follow Christ, I was sitting at Starbucks with Shawn and a few guys from church, my heart swelling with — you guessed it, pride. I was bragging on about how I was sharing my faith with my friends and taking a stand against sin, when, out of the corner of my eye, I noticed a middle-aged woman who was obviously upset.

She was sitting at a table by herself, her face was buried in her hands, and she was crying.

As the guys went on with their conversation, I couldn't take my eyes off this woman. Something deep within me was stirred with compassion.

"Fellas, you see that lady crying over there?" I pointed, trying not to be too conspicuous.

The guys turned and looked. "Man, that's too bad. I don't really know what we can do, though."

Our conversation continued, but I felt uneasy. A few minutes later, I looked over again. "Gosh, that lady is still crying back there, guys."

All of the sudden, the woman got up and began walking toward us on the way out the door. As she approached me, I felt like my heart was going to explode in my chest. It was as if the Holy Spirit inside me was lurching towards her, but I was at a loss to know what to do or say. Faced with the overwhelming reality that I had nothing to offer, I sat there frozen.

She walked by, still crying, got on a beach cruiser bike out front, and rode away.

In that moment, it was as if God's finger reached down from heaven and touched my heart. *You're not ready yet,* I sensed him saying. I immediately broke down in tears—a weepy, snotty mess—keenly aware of my weakness apart from God. The God of the Universe had just spoken into my life, and I was both devastated and in awe. I came face to face with how utterly weak my human courage was when it comes to spiritual things that truly matter.

Have you ever had an experience like this? You knew God was calling you to act, but pride got in the way. How would you want to respond differently next time?

Humility changes everything—the people we associate with, what we value, how we spend our time and money, and the countless decisions that make up our day-to-day lives. No longer are we self-absorbed or caught up in chasing the American Dream—being comfortable, happy, or having things go our way. A far greater dream has been opened to the eyes of our hearts—the dream of joining our Heavenly Father in spiritual warfare that sets other people free.

Recently, after a long weekend away speaking, I was eager to get home to Ashley and the kiddos, so I wasn't exactly thrilled to discover my connecting flight on Sunday night was cancelled. The longer I stood in line for the ticket counter, the more irritated I became.

You can't do this to me—I deserve better, I thought, particularly as the rumor spread down the line that the next available flight was Tuesday. TUESDAY?! I was about ready to burst. But then, I sensed God tugging at my heart, reminding me that every situation is an opportunity for him to show up. Taking a deep breath, I tried to calm down rather than freaking out, and pay attention to how God might be at work in this change of plans.

I struck up a conversation with a family standing close to me, who were equally frustrated. Before the night was out, we rented a van and hit the road for the seven-hour drive home. I felt a little bit giddy as we drove along, and I don't think it was from exhaustion.

Here we have seven hours together—what is God going to do?

As we talked about life and shared our stories, we began talking about faith, and I had the opportunity to share the gospel in a natural, relatable way. I can't take any credit here, because God swung open the door. My evening didn't go as planned *at all*—and that was beautiful.

Wow, God, it's just like you to do something like this, I reflected as I fell into bed late that night. Humility frees us to hold loosely to our plans, because we're grounded firmly in God. We know who we are, and who God is for us and in us. Moments of chaos, where things don't go our way, become exciting opportunities to watch for God at work and join in.

As long as you need approval from others, need your name to be known, or need people's applause, you are in bondage. But in Christ, the gut-wrenching angst of fear and shame are replaced with blood-pumping excitement.

The fear of the unknown becomes the anticipation of that which will be revealed.

Anxiety in the face of impossibility brings a giggle of wonder knowing the stage is set for a God-moment that will wow his audience.

Each opportunity to share the gospel turns into a "win" regardless of the earthly reaction or outcome. Every seed planted is a devastating blow in the war for souls. Each prayer prayed, each sin conquered, each act of generosity and love…it all matters. How can we unleash this dangerous power of the Holy Spirit? How can we stay humble in a world that constantly pulls us toward self-absorption?

Our answer is found in daily confession and repentance—walking in the freedom of God's forgiveness rather than shame and condemnation.

CHAPTER THREE

FORGIVEN AND SET FREE

God will never plant the seed of his life upon the soil of a hard, unbroken spirit…but only where the conviction of his Spirit has brought brokenness, where the soil has been watered with the tears of repentance as well as the tears of joy.
—*Alan Redpath*

THE ROOM WAS PITCH BLACK. Jerry couldn't even see his hand in front of his face, let alone the black belts circling him on every side.

"My heart beat out of my chest," Jerry vividly remembers. At any moment, the lights would flip off…then on again…and in that split second, as his eyes struggled to readjust to the black abyss, the attack would come.

From any angle. Without a second's warning.

Earning a black belt isn't for the faint of heart…but my friend Jerry is someone you don't want to mess with. The first time I met this guy, I was pretty intimidated. Jerry has a barrel chest, wild eyes, and a cinder-block-shaped head. Growing up on the streets, he's the definition of tough.

Thwack! A front kick came out of nowhere, hitting Jerry with full force in the face and sending him crashing to the ground. When Jerry came to, he was flat on his back, head pounding and the salty taste of blood in his mouth.

Surrounded by danger. Wounded. Helpless. Alone.

Sin puts you and I in a similar situation. The attacks of Satan often come when we least expect them—the enticement of pleasure, the desire to make a name for ourselves, the need to be right and prove our point—and we find ourselves knocked off our feet. Leveled by temptation. Guilt and shame hangs over us like a dark cloud, as if the lights of faith have gone out. It's hard to make sense of anything, let alone figure out how to fight back.

Ever been there? Inevitably, Satan whispers condemnation and hopelessness. *You'll never change. Look what a failure you are. I bet God doesn't want anything to do with you. He's ashamed. Angry. If he finds you, he'll certainly destroy you.*

In these moments, what we do *next* matters most.

How easy it is to follow in Adam and Eve's footsteps. Run…hide …make ourselves small and invisible. Nurse our wounds, justify our decisions, and cover up our failures. It's a trap, though—we end up in bondage to self-hatred and condemnation. Nothing brings Satan more glee than when followers of Jesus live as though the gospel isn't true.

Strategically, the devil's web of lies always leaves out the passionate, aggressive Father heart of God and the dangerous power of his forgiveness.

A RADICAL, PASSIONATE, CRAZY LOVE

Is God a cosmic killjoy? What kind of a God would condemn who I am? Who is he to forbid us from doing things we want—things that we think will make us happy? Our world often views God as a grumpy, authoritative parent who says, "It's my way or the highway." Or worse, we see him as a power-hungry tyrant: "Shut up and do what I say, or else."

But what if God hates sin so much because he loves us with a radical, passionate, crazy love? We often only see the pleasure of the moment, but from his perspective outside of time, God knows that sin will always leave us empty, robbing us of the life He intended for us as his children.

God hates sin like any good parent hates poisonous chemicals. If my two-year-old, Tess, found her way out to the garage, where the fertilizer and insect repellent are stored, I'd be there in an instant to step in and intervene. I'd scoop her up in my arms, pry the chemical container out of her grasp, and firmly tell her "no." Not because I want to hurt Tess or spoil her fun, but because I love her too much to let her destroy herself. Sure, she may kick and scream, convinced I am taking away something that she rightfully deserves. But I know what Tess can't yet grasp: the brightly colored bottles aren't toys. They're poison.

No matter how good it looks and feels, sin always poisons our souls. And I'm not just talking about the things we call "big" sins like sexual immorality, lying, intentionally hurting others, and the like. Sin can be anything we turn to instead of God for happiness and fulfillment—even things that look good from the outside.

God loves you too much to let you destroy yourself. That's why he can't stand idly by like a permissive, neglectful parent while Satan does his work to steal, kill, and destroy us (JN. 10:10). The moment I became a husband and father, I became exponentially more dangerous. Literally, every scenario I walk into, I'm looking for danger. That's because God has given me a bride and five precious little ones to take care of and protect. Anyone threatening my family needs to know that I have a black belt in crazy. This daddy is ready to fight!

So, when I'm standing in the supermarket and I'm holding a can of corn and you come around the corner, don't assume I haven't flipped the switch. If you look threatening, you had better beware. There could be corn flying.

I've thought through every scenario. At the gas station, if an assailant comes up to me, I'm going to pump five dollars' worth of gas in their eyes and follow that up with a roundhouse kick to their face. I will stop at nothing to make sure that my kids Lulu, Belle, Knox, Tess, and Piper are safe.

Satan's lies are often most dangerous because they contain an element of truth. He wants us to see just half of the reality: that God is holy and just…and wrathful. But what Satan hopes we will never grasp is that our Heavenly Father's aggression stems from love. God's heart to protect you is infinitely greater than my heart to protect my children. God is crazy about you. He wove every fiber of your DNA into existence and he treasures you. Because of this, he'll go up against sin in your life with a vengeance.

Countless times, I've turned away from God to other lovers to try to satisfy my soul. And Scripture reminds us, "[W]hoever keeps the whole law and yet stumbles at just one point is guilty of breaking all of it" (JAS. 2:9).

We've failed. You and I deserve separation from God forever. Satan will tell you that God is angry and out to get you: "The wrath of God is being revealed from heaven against all the godlessness and wickedness of people" (ROM. 1:18).

But that's only part of the story.

Yes, God is on a warpath — but it's not a warpath to destroy us. It's a battle to destroy Satan…and rescue us from the power of sin. The Crucifixion was a cosmic battle to redeem us by Jesus willingly offering himself as the object of God's wrath. Jesus stretched out his arms and in essence said, "I'll take it. Punish me, Father — and forgive them."

And his final cry before he died? *Tetelestai,* which in Greek means, "It is finished. It's over. It's done. Sin is defeated and Satan is powerless. My sons and daughters can now come home."[1] Here's how the Bible describes it in Colossians 2:13-15 (CEB):

> *When you were dead because of the things you had done wrong …God made you alive with Christ and forgave all the things you had done wrong. He destroyed the record of the debt we owed, with its requirements that worked against us. He canceled it by nailing it to the cross. When he disarmed the rulers and authorities, he exposed them to public disgrace.*

Did you catch that? The cross *destroyed* the record of our sin and *disarmed* Satan of his power. This beautiful devastation set us free to walk in the power of the Holy Spirit when we accept and live in God's forgiveness. Not just when we first choose to follow him, but every single day.

So often though, fear, pride, and false ideas about who God is get in the way.

GUT-WRENCHING DESIRE…FOR YOU

Sitting in the muddy stench of a pigpen, I imagine the prodigal son felt like he'd been hit with more than a few karate kicks (see

LK. 15). Having taken and squandered his inheritance, he was now empty, alone…and desperate. All of his best-laid plans had come to nothing.

With a hungry stomach and an aching soul, his mind drifted to his father. The one he had run from and disowned. The one who had never done anything but love and care for him.

"I will get up and go to my father…" (LK. 15:18) I believe this is where sin lost its power in the prodigal's life—not when he actually fell into his father's embrace, but when he saw through the glamor of sin and remembered who his father was. Compassionate. Gracious. Forgiving. When he mustered the little energy he had left and put one manure-covered foot in front of the other …turning toward home.

"The Lord is gracious and compassionate, slow to anger and rich in love…as far as the east is from the west, so far has he removed our transgressions from us" (PS. 145:8-9, 103:12). This is the only truth that will energize us to fight back against Satan's lies. It's hard to fully grasp the earth-shattering reality of God's forgiveness offered to us. We may assume he'll take us back with a slap on the wrist or a begrudging, "Well, I guess I have to—you're my kid."

But Scripture tells us that while the prodigal was still off in the distance, "[H]is father saw him and was filled with compassion for him; he ran to his son, threw his arms around him and kissed him" (LK. 15:20). The Greek word for "compassion" here—*splagchnizomai*—literally means "to be moved in the inward parts…to have the bowels yearn."[2] This speaks to a powerful gut reaction of desire and aching longing. Imagine all the love and desire you feel towards the person you are closest to, then multiply that by infinity.

That, my friend, is Jesus' heart toward you. He doesn't just tolerate you or begrudgingly acknowledge your existence. If you come home seeking forgiveness, you will not find God waiting in the living room with a stern eye and a wagging finger to give you a talking-to or a switching you'll never forget. "When you stray from his presence," Charles Stanley writes, "He longs for you to come back. He weeps that you are missing out on his love, protection, and provision. He throws his arms open, runs toward you, gathers you up, and welcomes you home."[3]

It's extreme…incomprehensible, really. Forgiveness like this defies everything many of us have ever known or experienced in human relationships. Do you believe that God will take you back—really truly, at the core of your being? Do you *get* how much he loves you, how he aches for you to come to him? Or do you doubt, like I so often do?

Maybe you wonder if you've out-sinned his grace. Or maybe life seems pretty good, and you struggle to admit how desperately you need him. In one way or another, we are all prodigals. We've stiff-armed God, ignored him, or actively fought against him, trying to do life our own way. And we do this not just once, but over and over again. As Henri Nouwen reflects, "I am the prodigal every time I search for unconditional love where it cannot be found."[4]

That's why accepting and living in God's forgiveness isn't just a one-time thing when we choose to follow Jesus. It's a daily posture of repentance and dependence. It's remembering who our Father is whenever we fail and guilt blocks out the light of grace.

Don't let Satan fool you. "The gospel is this," Tim and Kathy Keller reflect. "We are more sinful and flawed in ourselves than we ever dared believe, yet at the very same time we are more loved and accepted in Jesus Christ than we ever dared hope."[5]

Humility, as we explored in the last chapter, paves the way for us to accept God's life-altering forgiveness. And this forgiveness releases the power of the Holy Spirit in our lives.

"In Christ, you are fully forgiven, freely forgiven, and forever forgiven," Matt Chandler reminds us. He continues,

> *You have no sin . . . past, present, and future . . . that has more power than the cross of Jesus Christ. None. This means your salvation wasn't just a past event alone, but that Christ even now is continuing to save you. He didn't forgive your past sins and is now leaving it up to you to conquer present and future sins. He paid for it all . . . God is not watching where you are now, watching how you stumble and fall, and regretting the decision to pay the price for you in full. He doesn't regret saving you.*[6]

Take a moment to soak in this reality of the gospel for you. It changes everything. Not just at the moment of your salvation, but every time you fail and fall short. Jesus longs to forgive, heal, and welcome you home.

Will you fall into his arms? Or do you feel the frantic urge to try and scrub away the muck of the pigpen first?

YOU DON'T NEED TO CLEAN YOURSELF UP

Drying my son Knox off after bath time is a lot like wrestling a warthog. One night, when he was about two, Knox was especially energetic and eager to run around the living room to "air dry." Wriggling to get down, he slipped free of my grasp, but it wasn't his feet that hit the tile floor — it was his face.

Knox's four front teeth disappeared like prairie dogs up into his gums. The poor little guy screamed out in pain and panic as his mouth filled with blood.

How does a loving father respond in moments like this?

"See what happens when you don't listen? Go clean yourself up. And learn your lesson!"

Far from it! As best as I know, a loving father swoops in to rescue and help. I got down on Knox's level, right in the middle of the blood and snot and messiness. I scooped up my little boy and put his head on my chest, so he could hear my heartbeat.

"You're okay, buddy. I've got you. I'm sorry it hurts. We'll get you cleaned up."

Knox's ear-piercing screams slowed. A few minutes later, he wiggled out of my arms and took off running to make his lap around the living room. Tear streaks still on his face and his teeth in hibernation, but somehow, Knox knew that everything was going to be okay.

This is a beautiful picture of how God takes us when we come to him. Naked. Vulnerable. Wounded. Bleeding. Our attempts at being good on our own all jacked up.

Depending on your own experiences growing up, this might be hard to comprehend. Perhaps your parents expected you to clean yourself up — be a good kid — do the right thing. In an instance like I just described, maybe you would have been disciplined, made to clean up the blood on the floor, and harshly reprimanded on the way to the dentist's office.

God is not like this. There is no circumstance where your loving Heavenly Father isn't ready and waiting to scoop you up in his arms and offer comfort, forgiveness, and healing. But we've got to take the first step to come to him—messy, imperfect, acknowledging our need for his grace and forgiveness.

As followers of Jesus, sin in our lives doesn't create an eternal separation from God, but it does create a relational separation. When I wriggle out of my Father's arms and try to go my own way, things get messy real fast. In that moment when Knox was hurt, denying it wouldn't fix anything. If, with all the courage a two-year-old can muster, Knox tried to dry his tears, push through the pain, and move on with our evening routine—well, it wouldn't work. If not attended to, wounds can fester and become infected. The same is true of our hearts. When we sin—and ignore it—our hearts fester with guilt and condemnation before a holy God. Our faith gets infected with lies and our souls soon become numb to the prompting of the Holy Spirit.

When we are in Christ, Satan cannot ultimately hurt us, but he can make us ineffective. He can trip us up by making us think that we need to clean ourselves up and pull ourselves together before coming to God. It's a bold-faced lie that keeps us in bondage. Unconfessed sin is the stomping grounds of our enemy. And repenting and accepting God's forgiveness is the salve that heals our hearts and restores our intimacy with God.

I like to call it the *Vacate Principle.*

THE FREEDOM OF REPENTANCE

When you go on vacation, what happens to your home? It's vacant—left empty. All the flesh leaves the house. This is the essence of the Vacate Principle—every single day, God calls us to empty ourselves of our flesh so that we can be filled with the Holy Spirit.

Even as followers of Jesus, you and I still struggle with our sinful natures. "I don't really understand myself," Paul writes, "for I want to do what is right, but I don't do it. Instead, I do what I hate"

(ROM. 7:15, NLT). Left to ourselves, we'll inevitably screw things up. You and I need Jesus—every moment of every day.

"[T]hose who belong to Christ Jesus have crucified the flesh with its passions and desires" (GAL. 5:24). This is not a one-time event—it's a daily discipline. As I rub the sleep out of my eyes each morning, I try to humble my heart before God, ask him to reveal my sin, and seek his forgiveness.

In order to be used by God, we need him to move the junk out of the way—our selfishness, pride, insecurities, fear, and need to be right. We need him to clean house…to vacate our flesh.

In Psalm 139, David gives us a model of how this works: "Search me, God, and know my heart; test me and know my anxious thoughts. See if there is any offensive way in me, and lead me in the way everlasting" (PS. 139:23-24). Similarly, the author of Lamentations encourages, "Why should any living mortal, or any man, offer complaint in view of his own sins? Let us examine and probe our ways, and let us return to the LORD. We lift up our heart and hands toward God in heaven" (LAM. 3:39-41, NASB).

When you seek God and ask him to clean house in your soul, be ready for him to point some things out. It's hard to admit that we're wrong. That we've screwed up for the umpteenth time. That no matter how long we've been following Jesus, we never move beyond grace and repentance. Luther began his Ninety-five Theses with this assertion: "When our Lord and Master Jesus Christ said, 'Repent' (MT. 4:17), he willed the entire life of believers to be one of repentance."[7]

Just like my kids need a bath after a day of playing outside, our hearts need perpetual cleansing. I believe the reason that so many Christians are walking around without spiritual power today is because they accepted Christ's forgiveness twenty years ago and thought they were "good to go." But the reality is this: if you don't take a bath for a week, or a month, or a year, you are going to start to stink.

"If we claim to have fellowship with him and yet walk in the darkness, we lie and do not live out the truth. But if we walk in the light, as he is in the light, we have fellowship with one another, and the blood of Jesus, his Son, purifies us from all sin" (1 JN. 1:6-7).

There is amazing freedom in bringing your sins, failures, and weaknesses into the light of God's truth. No more hiding, minimizing or pretending. No more trying to heal yourself. He promises not just to forgive, but also to purify you from every single sin.

Vacating our hearts is the process of coming to God each day—asking for forgiveness and seeking repentance. When we do that, that wall of relational separation is obliterated by grace. While it may be painful in the moment, so much wonderful fruit comes as a result. The best way I can describe the Vacate Principle is by drawing it out:

RELATIONAL GROWTH/CLOSENESS WITH GOD

I'm not an award-winning artist, but here's the gist of it. As you and I humble ourselves before God and cultivate an attitude of daily repentance, something mysterious happens — our intimacy with him grows. We find ourselves falling in love with Jesus more and more.

The closer we get to God, the more we catch glimpses of who he really is, and the more we see our need for and desperate dependence on him. No longer do we need to brag about our own accomplishments, ministry successes, or personal talents. His love, mercy, and forgiveness are so overwhelming that they press our faces into the carpet of humility.

As our posture changes, we are slowly transformed to become more like Jesus — more holy, more loving, more patient, more forgiving. His commands are no longer burdensome (1 JN. 5:3). What was formerly a pain in the neck now becomes a joy and a privilege because we understand God's grace, love and his plan — and we get to be part of it. Daily abiding and diligent pursuit of God develops powerful, potent, and dangerous faith.

FORGIVING OURSELVES, FORGIVING OTHERS

I'll never forget meeting Jason. This guy spoke with wisdom and spiritual authority. Aside from his prison garb, you never would have guessed his history. Sitting in a circle with Jason and his buddies, we wrestled with the concept of forgiveness. Many of these men were former murderers or drug dealers. They were locked up—behind bars—but these brothers in Christ grasped the forgiveness of God in a big way. They knew how sinful and evil their hearts were and how desperately they needed grace.

"The things we've done, Shay," one guy spoke up, "that's where we get hung up. I replay the murders in my head every single day. They haunt me—the ways I caused torment, pain, and suffering. It's unspeakable." His voice trailed off. "How do we forgive ourselves?"

Maybe you've been there, too. You *get* the fact that God offers unconditional love and forgiveness, but you hate yourself. You despise every fiber of your being because of the ways you've failed, screwed up your life, and hurt others.

I sat by as Jason poured truth into his brother: "Withholding forgiveness from yourself, it's like stiff-arming the God of the Universe, saying that Jesus' sacrifice wasn't enough. There is literally *nothing*—not even the most heinous crime—that God is not eager to forgive."

That day, I witnessed a group of tough convicts fall into God's arms and beg him to restore their broken selves, to free them from self-hatred and enable them to grasp their true identity—not as convicts, but as his beloved sons. Worshipping and praying with these men was an honor. Their passion to seek the face of God was infectious and their unabashed desperation for forgiveness brought me to tears. Despite the shackles on their wrists, these brothers are more free and spiritually alive than many people who have never even gotten a speeding ticket.

In the upside-down kingdom of God, we are all vagabonds and criminals, all equally in need of God's grace. It is this reality—this vision of just how earth-shattering God's forgiveness is—that empowers us to forgive ourselves and others. In the words of Martin

Luther, "If anyone insists on his own goodness and despises others, let him look into himself...he will find he is no better than the others and that in the presence of God, everyone must duck his head and come into the joy of forgiveness only through the low door of humility."[8]

When we have been wronged, violated, or taken advantage of, rushing to say "I forgive you" without feeling and grieving the full weight of the loss we've experienced can be self-destructive. But harboring bitterness isn't the answer either.

Corrie ten Boom's life is a powerful example. During World War II, Corrie and her family were arrested for hiding Jews. Corrie and her sister Betsie were sent to Ravensbruck, an all-female concentration camp where 96,000 women died or were killed. As Betsie wasted away from malnutrition and disease, she had three visions from God, which she shared with Corrie:

To create a house for former prisoners and help them rehabilitate.

To own a concentration camp and transform it into a place to teach Germans to love.

To travel the world sharing how she had experienced God while at Ravensbruck.

As Betsie breathed her last, she begged Corrie, "Tell them what we have learned here. Tell them that there is no pit so deep that [God's love] is not deeper still."[9] One week before all the women her age were to be killed, Corrie was released due to a clerical error.

Three years later, after the war was over, God called her to go back to Germany and share the message of God's forgiveness and grace. After speaking at a church in Munich, Corrie was approached by a man whose face seemed vaguely familiar. In an instant, it all came rushing back—he had been a Nazi guard at Ravensbruck. She remembered feeling angry, ashamed, and terrified as she and Betsie were forced to walk past him naked at their arrival to the concentration camp.

"You mentioned Ravensbruck in your talk," he said. "I was a guard in there...but since that time, I have become a Christian... will you forgive me?"[10]

Corrie stood there in shock as he held out his hand. How could she forgive this man who had tormented them and played a role in

Betsie's tragic death? Knowing that it was impossible in her own strength, she cried out to God: "I can lift my hand, I can do that much. You supply the feeling."[11]

Though her heart was still cold, Corrie grasped the man's hand in obedient expectation, declaring, "I forgive you, brother! With all my heart!"[12] As she did, a miraculous thing happened. A healing current rushed down her arm, into their firm grasp, and spread throughout her whole body as she was moved to tears.

"I have never known God's love so intensely as I did then," Corrie remembers.[13] In that moment, God did something only he could do — unite a former Nazi guard and prisoner as brother and sister in Christ.

It is difficult, if not humanly impossible, to forgive those who have committed evil against us. It may not always be an instantaneous experience, but rather a slow process of healing and inner transformation. Regardless, forgiveness is always supernatural, and it is incredibly dangerous to Satan's evil schemes.

FROM POWERLESS PRISONERS TO DANGEROUS WARRIORS

If you find your spiritual walk shallow or powerless, stop and reflect for a moment. *What might be separating you from the power God has given you access to through the Holy Spirit?*

Don't buy the lies of Satan. You cannot save or fix or even clean up yourself. Come to Jesus exactly as you are. Confess your sin. Accept his forgiveness. Turn away from temptation. Soak your soul in his gut-wrenching desire and love for you. This will free you to forgive yourself and others who might have hurt you. It will free you to live abundantly.

Every time we repent and accept God's forgiveness, we swing wide the door of our hearts to be filled with the Holy Spirit (EPH. 5:18). We get to camp out in the too-good-to-be-true-but-true realities of God's grace, mercy, and love. And *this* is what has the power to transform us from fearful prisoners into dangerous warriors.

I love how Alan Redpath puts it:

> *It is Satan's delight to tell me that once he's got me, he will keep me. But at that moment I can go back to God. And I know that if I confess my sins, God is faithful and just to forgive me...[We can] return to the battle again, no longer trusting in the false and insufficient human resources which so foolishly we had taken into the battle, but now trusting in the limitless resources of our risen Lord.*[14]

The daily posture of confession and repentance makes us dangerous, because they unite us with Christ, so his power can work in and through us. So the next time you find yourself splayed out on the floor, your head pounding with shame and the taste of failure fresh in your mouth, remember this—his forgiveness is there for the taking.

Crawl, **limp**, cry out — **do whatever you need to** — **in order to get to Jesus**.

Remember the story of Jerry? When the master black belt flipped the light on, my buddy was square on his feet. Ready to fight. His fists were out, his jaw clenched with more grit and determination than ever before.

Forgiveness unleashes the power of the Holy Spirit to get us back on our feet, gives us strength to stand firm against evil, and empowers us to do damage with the Sword of the Spirit.

What kind of damage? Let's take a look.

A NOTE FROM THE AUTHOR

I pray that God is stirring your heart as you read! I would like to offer you another tool that will help you grow in your intimacy with Jesus. Email dangerouschristian@gmail.com and we will send you a free Dangerous Christian Bible Study.

Your Friend,
Shay

DANGEROUS

PURSUIT

CHAPTER FOUR

THE SWORD OF THE SPIRIT

The Bible is not an end in itself, but a means to bring men to an intimate and satisfying knowledge of God, that they may enter into him…may delight in his presence, may taste and know the inner sweetness of the very God himself in the core and center of their hearts.
—*A. W. Tozer*

JAKE THE SNAKE WAS A TOWERING MOUNTAIN OF A MAN. I was envious of his tree trunk torso, his long, curly mullet, and his sprawling chest hair. It was the kind of chest hair thirteen-year-old boys only dreamed of—so manly that when you put a shirt over it, it would inevitably spring through the fabric.

This WWF wrestler was the epitome of strength, and my dad, brother, and I sat mesmerized many a Sunday afternoon in front of the TV, watching every swing, hook, and uppercut. Jake was unstoppable, and his opponents never lasted long before they teetered and fell unconscious to the mat.

And then came the best part. Jake always pulled out a giant, ten-foot python and draped it over his defeated rival's body.

This, I decided, *was real manhood.*

When I found out that Jake the Snake was speaking at summer camp, I was out of my mind with excitement. My buddies and I were the first in line for chapel, pumping quarters into the soda machine and smashing root beer over our heads in anticipation of meeting one of the greatest wrestlers in the world. We rushed in to get the best seats, sticky from head to toe.

I had barely slept the night before, and lying in bed, I'd made a plan. I would sit up front, and the moment Jake the Snake pulled that python out, I would reach out and touch the beast…regardless of whether or not it cost me my hand.

I held my breath, waiting for the pyrotechnics, smoke machines, and lasers that would inevitably precede Jake's entrance. When a rather ordinary-looking dude walked out on stage, dressed in brown leather shoes, khaki pants, and a plaid shirt, I was more than a little confused.

Jake didn't have even a single chest hair popping out through his shirt. He had cut his mullet, too, and there was no python in sight. Everything awesome about Jake the Snake was gone. I was crushed, and to this day, I don't remember a word Jake said in sharing his testimony.

As Jake finished up whatever he was saying, a nerdy pastor-looking guy came be-bopping down the aisle. Imagine a Christian version of Ross Geller from *Friends*, and you get the picture. Apparently he was "part two" of our chapel lineup. He opened up a huge Bible and I rolled my eyes.

Who is this joker? Are you kidding me? I thought. *I could pin him on the floor easily.*

Soon, though, I found myself living in the middle of a story he brought to life from Scripture. We were preparing for battle alongside thirty of the greatest warriors of Israel. Among all of King David's soldiers, the most infamous were "The Three" — three mighty men who had become legends. The mere mention of their names struck fear in the hearts of the Philistines: Josheb-Basshebeth. Shammah. Eleazar.

Especially Eleazar.

In the middle of a battle, the rest of the soldiers chickened out, tucked tail and ran, but Eleazar stood his ground in a field of barley: "He rose and struck down the Philistines until his hand was weary, and his hand clung to the sword. And the LORD brought about a great victory that day…" (2 SAM. 23:10, ESV). Eleazar was a beast, I decided. I was ready to time travel — to fight by his side and put those Philistines in their place. Give me a sword, and I'd fight to the death, too! In all my youthful zeal, what I didn't yet grasp was that my sword was ready and waiting. To live dangerously, all I needed to do was pick it up, learn how to wield it, and cling to it.

MORE THAN JUST A BOOK

I'm the proud owner of the Claymore, a life-sized replica of William Wallace's sword. It's massive—over four feet long—and I'll be honest, the thought of carrying it into battle is a little bit unnerving due to its size. If you ever come to Kanakuk Kamps, you might get to see the Claymore in action, but most of the time, it stands in my office as a reminder.

In ancient Israel, owning a weapon wasn't about being cool or hip. It was about survival. There was no calling 911, no sheriff ready to rush to the scene. Without a sword, you and I would be completely powerless—vulnerable to attack and unable to defend ourselves. In Eleazar's day, we would likely have slept with our sword close by, perhaps even gripping its hilt to be prepared to fight at a moment's notice.

As soon as our feet hit the floor in the morning, the first thing we'd instinctually do (before checking our phone or making coffee!) would be to fasten our belt and scabbard, literally strapping that sword to our body. Wherever we went—whatever the day held—our sword was there, hanging by our side. Within arm's reach. Ready to counter any attack.

Eleazar's sword wasn't just a weapon or a tool. It was a part of him. "[H]is hand clung to the sword," the Bible tells us (2 SAM. 23:10, ESV). The Hebrew word for "clung" here is *dabaq*, which literally means to be joined together with, to abide in, to hold fast to.[1] It's the same word used in Genesis 2:24 when God commands a husband to "cleave to his wife"—to become one flesh. It shows up in Deuteronomy 11:22 when we are commanded to "love the LORD your God, listen to his voice, and hold fast to him" and again when the psalmist cries out, "I cling to you; your right hand upholds me" (PS. 63:8).

In the spiritual battle raging just beyond our senses, our greatest weapon is "the sword of the Spirit, which is the word of God" (EPH. 6:17). Yet we can only stand firm like Eleazar when this weapon becomes a part of us—secured firmly to our waist with the belt of truth.

Maybe you, like me, have been guilted or browbeaten into reading your Bible more. We're told it is the handbook for life, and holds the answers to all of our questions, but this can easily reduce Scripture to a list of "dos and don'ts"—a moral code that we are supposed to follow. How easy it is to skim through a chapter, tweet a verse, and move on with our day—to reduce time in God's Word to a line in our to-do list.

Perhaps the greatest lie we believe about Scripture is that it is just a book—words on a page written by a bunch of spiritual guys inspired by God thousands of years ago. Could it be that we've missed the heart of God's revelation to us?

"In the beginning was the Word," John writes, "and the Word was with God, and the Word was God" (JN. 1:1). Long before one verse of the Bible was ever written, Jesus Christ was the expression of the thoughts of God. That's what *Word* means here—the *logos*.[2]

It is an incomprehensible mystery. Jesus himself as the Word of God. And with his incarnation and life on this earth, "The Word became flesh and made his dwelling among us" (JN. 1:14). In God's providence, he has given us the written word of Scripture, but ink on a page is not in itself transformative. Instead, through the illumination of the Holy Spirit, the Bible becomes a gateway to experiencing the true Word of God—Jesus himself. I love how A.W. Tozer explains it:

> *The Bible is the written word of God, and because it is written it is confined and limited by the necessities of ink and paper and leather. The Voice of God, however, is alive and free as the sovereign God is free. 'The words that I speak unto you, they are spirit, and they are life.' The life is in the speaking words. God's word in the Bible can have power only because it corresponds to God's Word in the universe. It is the present Voice which makes the written word powerful. Otherwise it would lie locked in slumber within the covers of a book.*[3]

C. S. Lewis's allegorical tale, *The Lion, The Witch and The Wardrobe,* offers a beautiful picture of how we can experience God through Scripture. Just as the wardrobe became a gateway for Peter, Susan, Edmund, and Lucy to enter the world of Narnia, so the work of the Holy Spirit through Scripture is our point of access to

THE SWORD OF THE SPIRIT

knowing God. Without the enlightenment of the Holy Spirit, we will face a dead end, as the children did when they tried to return to Narnia later, and were disappointed to find only an ordinary wardrobe with a solid wood back. We cannot find intimacy with God when we approach Scripture through a purely intellectual or human mindset. Its truths remain "locked in slumber"—outside of our reach.

Satan is not worried when we spend a few minutes flipping through the Bible, looking for good advice or rules to live by. After all, this is how the Pharisees approached Scripture—as "a source of trivia for life's dilemmas," Michael Horton reflects.[4] Their questions to Jesus were always aimed at using biblical knowledge to categorize, judge, and criticize. How easy it is to get lost in Biblicism, forgetting that "the primary purpose of reading the Bible is not to know the Bible, but to know God," James Merritt reminds us.[5] Dangerous Christians do more than read or even memorize Scripture, they meet God through it, and are changed by him.

Do you feel like you've been stuck in a wardrobe—banging against its solid wood back, looking for a way into the Narnia of God's presence? Let this reality set you free from legalism and striving: God has given you the Holy Spirit to "guide you into all the truth" (JN. 16:13). He desires for you to know him intimately and experientially—to cling to him—not just know theological ideas *about* him.

"Do not be conformed to the pattern of this world," the apostle Paul encourages, "but be transformed by the renewing of your mind" (ROM. 12:2). Working in tandem with the Word of God, the Holy Spirit has the power to transform us from the inside out,.

How do you approach God's Word? As a spiritual duty? Or as an opportunity to fall more deeply in love?

FALLING IN LOVE

"The Holy Scriptures are our letters from home," Saint Augustine reflects.[6] When Josh went to boot camp, he wasn't allowed access to the outside world by phone, e-mail, Skype, Facebook—nothing—for three months! But he could receive letters. Without fail, his then fiancée (now wife) Bethany would write him every week, sharing her daily experiences and dreaming on paper about their future together.

From hundreds of miles away, Bethany cheered him on and encouraged him to persevere through all the challenges of military training. She attempted to put down in words her passionate love and desire for him.

"Those letters became a lifeline for me," Josh shared. "Knowing that she was waiting for me at the end, that she loved and believed in me — it enabled me to keep going when my body was exhausted and I was ready to give up.

"In some mysterious way, Bethany was with me. Even though I was on the other side of the country, our hearts were united."

Imagine Bethany's love for her fiancé times a million — and that does not even begin to scratch the surface of the passionate desire out of which God inspired the words of Scripture.

It's easy to get caught up in the day-to-day stresses of life and forget that this world is not our home. Our Heavenly Father aches and longs, with all of creation, for our return to the true Eden, where all things will be redeemed and made right. Where rather than glimpses and glimmers of his glory, we will see him face to face and be united with him forever.

This understanding of the Bible has changed everything for me. No longer is reading and memorizing Scripture something I *should* do to be a "good" Christian. No longer is the Bible just a list of God's commands and rules. Instead, this book I hold in my hands mysteriously contains an interstellar message from the Lover of my soul.

Somehow, through the power of the Holy Spirit in us, as we read the Bible, God is reaching across space and time to woo and pursue our hearts and whisper of his love and mercy. To tell us the truth about who we are and all that he is for us. Søren Kierkegaard writes,

> *To read the Bible as God's word one must read it with his heart in his mouth, on tip-toe, with eager expectancy, in conversation with God. To read the Bible thoughtlessly or carelessly or academically or professionally is not to read the*

Bible as God's Word. As one reads it as a love letter is read,
then one reads it as the Word of God.[7]

Sometimes it's difficult to understand what it really means to build an intimate relationship with an invisible God. After all, we can't go on a date, grab coffee, or catch a movie with God — can we?

Consider a significant relationship in your life. Maybe it's a parent, a friend, or a spouse. For me, I think about getting to know my wife Ashley. When we first met, I found myself curious and drawn to her. Ashley exuded the joy of the Lord. She was beautiful inside and out. And her southern accent, blue eyes, and blonde hair captivated me. So I mustered up all the courage I had and asked her on a date.

On the way to pick her up, I was all nerves — I really liked this girl and didn't want to mess it up! We started out with dinner at Big Cedar, one of my favorite restaurants. Then, I had arranged for a buddy of mine who is a pilot to take us on a prop airplane ride over the Ozarks. It sounded romantic in theory, but what I didn't know at the time in was that Ashley gets easily airsick. We survived the airplane ride, and I spent the next few hours nursing her back to health. Talk about a memorable evening!

It wasn't the perfect date, but one thing was certain: I wanted to go out with her again. So I asked. And thankfully, she said yes.

After a long day at work, I couldn't wait to spend time together. To unwind, commiserate about the hard moments, and share in the joyous ones. To laugh, or maybe cry, but most of all just to be together. To make memories. Explore new places. And go on adventures.

I was intrigued by Ashley, pulled toward her like a magnet. The more I knew her, the more I longed to spend time with her — the more I fell in love.

Slowly, I began to realize I didn't want to go through life without this woman who had stolen my heart, so I asked Ashley to be my wife. That was ten years ago, and since then we've built a life together — we've brought beautiful children into the world and endured many a sleepless night; we've held each other and wept over the death of loved ones; we've fought through conflict to stay engaged with each other's hearts.

My relationship with Ashley has changed me in some pretty dramatic ways. Her intimate presence in my life has exposed my shortcomings and, at the same time, covered them in love. The same is true with us and God. It's easy to over-spiritualize things and forget that we are made in God's image. The yearnings, desires, and longings we feel in dating and marriage are just a pale reflection of the ultimate romance. A relationship that, unlike any other in this world, has not been tainted by selfishness and sin.

Jesus knows everything about us and yet still pursues, cherishes, and treasures us as his bride. He is the greatest Romancer of all time: "I have loved you with an everlasting love; I have drawn you with unfailing kindness" (JER. 31:3). The devil trembles when we grasp our true identity as the beloved children of God. We become dangerous when we understand Scripture as not just a book, but an invitation to know and be known by God.

NOURISHMENT FOR OUR SOULS

If there's one thing I've learned being a parent, it's that babies don't have any problem being desperate and dependent, looking to their mom and dad (well, let's be honest—mostly mom) to meet every single need they have, day or night. Infants don't get the concept of maintaining their composure or trying to pull themselves up by their own bootstraps. If Piper is hungry or has a wet diaper or is feeling out of sorts, she is going to let Mom and Dad know. Let me tell you, that girl has some lungs on her!

The apostle Peter admonishes us to come to God with this same desperation: "Like newborn babies, crave pure spiritual milk, so that by it you may grow up in your salvation, now that you have tasted that the Lord is good" (1 PET. 2:2-3). This image of being nourished by God's Word and gaining spiritual "muscle" echoes back to Jeremiah 15:16, where the prophet exclaims, "When I discovered your words, I devoured them. They are my joy and my heart's delight" (NLT). Crave...devour...grow up. Scripture isn't just a nice appetizer to our life in the Spirit. It is the main course—the source of our spiritual nourishment.

When the New Testament talks about the Word of God, one

of two Greek words is used — *logos* or *rhéma*. While *logos* refers to the expression of the thoughts of God through Scripture, *rhéma* is "that which is or has been uttered by the living voice."[8] It's the spoken word of God. Countering Satan's temptation in the wilderness, Jesus proclaimed, "Man shall not live on bread alone, but by every [*rhéma*] that comes from the mouth of God" (MT. 4:4, emphasis mine).

Have you ever had a "light bulb" moment when you were reading Scripture — something you'd read hundreds of times jumped out at you, impacting you in a new way? The Holy Spirit reveals to us the rhéma of God beyond the *logos* written on the page.

This is the Word that is "living and active, sharper than any two-edged sword, piercing to the division of soul and of spirit, of joints and of marrow, and discerning the thoughts and intentions of the heart" (HEB. 4:12, ESV). It has supernatural ability to nourish our souls and grow our faith, even in the midst of great hardship.

Just ask Brother Yun. Born in Communist China, Yun grew up in a culture devoid of Christianity. Every Bible had been gathered up by the government and burned. Yun's mother had heard the gospel and accepted Christ as a young child, but over years of communist rule, her faith had all but evaporated.

When Yun was sixteen years old, his father was diagnosed with an aggressive form of cancer, and his body began to waste away. One night, in desperation, his mother remembered her childhood faith, gathered the family together, and prayed to Jesus for healing.

Supernaturally, Yun's father's health was restored. There was no other explanation but God — a God who had been exiled from the culture, but who was present by his Spirit, ready and eager to respond to the cries of his children.

Yun's parents called together their extended family, who came dressed in black, expecting a funeral. They were in shock when Yun's father opened the door to welcome them, healthy and strong. The witness of this miracle brought many in the family to Jesus, but they knew little of this God who had moved so powerfully.

All of his life, Yun had been taught in school that God did not exist — but here before his eyes, he witnessed a very different reality. This teenage boy began to fast and pray, begging God to bring him a Bible, so he could know more. One night, he dreamed that he met two men with a red bag over their shoulder. They pulled a Bible from the bag and gave it to him.

Yun awoke with a start, believing that perhaps God had finally answered his prayer. He scoured the house in vain, and broke down weeping when he realized it was only a dream. Just then, Yun's family was startled by a knock at the door.

Outside stood two men with a red sack. One of the men reached inside, pulled out a Bible, and handed it to Yun. Then they vanished into the night. It was yet another miracle.

Yun devoured the Word of God. After reading it cover to cover, he began memorizing a chapter from the Book of Matthew each day. Before long, the news leaked out to neighbors and friends that Yun's father had been miraculously healed…and that a Bible had been discovered.

People were intrigued and they asked to meet with Yun to hear more. The boy dare not take the Bible with him, lest he be caught. At the arranged meeting place, Yun found the majority of his small community—close to forty people—packed in a house.

Unsure of what else to say, he quoted the twenty-eight chapters of Matthew that he had memorized. According to Yun's testimony, every person there came to faith that night! Yun was just an ordinary teenager.[9] But he was hungry to know and experience God for himself, gobbling up an entire book of Scripture and becoming a vessel through which the Holy Spirit could transform not only his, but also others', lives.

LIGHT FOR OUR PATH

When kids come to camp at Kanakuk, one of my favorite things to do is take them spelunking. It sounds exotic, but in reality, we spend most of the time crawling on our hands and knees through tight spaces, mud, and rough terrain—making our way down into the caves and caverns of the Ozarks.

Once we get hundreds of feet back in, I encourage everyone to turn off their headlamps, and we sit there for a few minutes, taking in the reality of the thick darkness that surrounds us. The reality is, without those headlamps, we would likely die in there. We'd have no chance of safely navigating the narrow pathways and precipices and mazes of tunnels to find our way out.

The same is true in life. In this topsy-turvy world, things can get pretty confusing sometimes. Pretty dark. Pretty scary. Yet the same God who said "let there be light" and brought order and beauty out of chaos longs to shed his light in our hearts (GEN. 1:3).

"Your word is a lamp to guide my feet and a light for my path," the psalmist reflects (PS. 119:105, NLT). Have you ever tripped over something in the dark before? Maybe it wasn't in a cave; perhaps you were trying to find your way to the bathroom in the middle of the night. Most of the time, I have a strange knack for attending to our kids' needs only half-awake, but I've also been known to misjudge the doorway and walk smack-dab into the wall.

A light, even the little LED on my phone, changes everything. It protects me and brings so much clarity. Sure, it may not light up the whole room, but it illuminates my next step.

"The Bible is no mere book," Napoleon Bonaparte is quoted as saying, "but a Living Creature…"[10] More than just a historical account, every story in the Bible is a snapshot of God at work—the same God we know and follow, who does not change. We need these pictures, these stories, these examples as illumination to help us remember…

The Redeemer who provided for Adam and Eve by covering their nakedness (GEN. 3) and forgave David for murder and adultery (2 SAM. 12) is eager to forgive and heal our brokenness.

The Rescuer who parted the Red Sea and led his people out in freedom (EX. 13), who delivered Daniel from the lion's den (DAN. 6), is all-powerful to protect and deliver us when all seems lost.

The Restorer who brought good from Joseph's imprisonment in Egypt (GEN. 50) and joy from Ruth's mourning (RUTH 4) is at work in the midst of our trials and shattered dreams.

Where do you find yourself in the grand, eternal story of God at work across history? Is it in Jacob's struggle with God? Hannah's aching desire to be a mother? Moses' burden of leading God's people? Jonah's urge to run from God? Martha's performance-oriented mindset? Peter's at-times thoughtless passion?

As I read these stories with my kids and see the wonder in their eyes, I pray that they never lose this sense of curiosity and awe—and I pray to cultivate it, too. I pray for the *rhéma* of these stories to illuminate our hearts.

It's one thing to read God's Word; it's another to let the Word read us. To cry out to the same God who blessed Jacob, who answered Hannah's prayer, who gave Moses wisdom, who forgave Jonah and gave him a fresh start, who freed Martha from the slavery of striving, who loved Peter just as he was. This is the same God who is eager to intervene in our lives and circumstances with exactly the same power.

Satan will do everything he can to discourage and distract you from this reality. He knows full well that dwelling in Jesus will transform you and I into bold and courageous warriors who don't just read Scripture, but devour it like Brother Yun did—as our daily nourishment, our identity, our spiritual DNA.

Living in these truths makes us a threat to the enemy because we are in Christ and he is in us (1 JN. 4:13). All we have to do is come to our Heavenly Father with the simple faith of a child, saying, like Samuel, "Speak, Lord, for your servant is listening," and then quiet our hearts to listen for the *rhéma* (1 SAM. 3:10). This Word has divine power to shape us into men and women who know without a doubt who and *whose* we are.

Men and women who are dangerous, finding strength and confidence in the face of spiritual attack because we cling to the Word with the same intensity that Eleazar clung to his sword.

How do we cultivate this kind of spiritual strength? It starts with seeking.

CHAPTER FIVE

SEEKING GOD

God is always seeking you. Every sunset. Every clear blue sky. Each ocean wave. The starry hosts of night. He blankets each new day with the invitation, "I am here."
—*Louie Giglio*

As a little boy, I loved to follow my dad around the farm in my diaper and muck boots. I often clamored up the fence to watch Dad feed the cattle, and crawled into Grandpa's lap every chance I got to help him drive the tractor.

Growing up in my early years on a Midwest family farm, we didn't have much, but we had everything we needed. Every day was an adventure waiting to happen.

Once our chores were done, my brother and I would take off exploring as long as the sun lasted. Ordinary hay bales became treacherous mazes to be navigated. Scrap lumber was transformed into intimidating fortresses, and giant oak trees served as lookouts for the enemy.

We tied logs together with scraps of rope and set sail down the creek in our makeshift raft, harvesting buckets of wild blackberries from the briars that lined the fields. We spent many an afternoon hunting, bursting with pride to show off our bounty as we traipsed home for dinner.

Sweaty, exhausted, covered with dust and chiggers. Not a care in the world, except fueling up for another day and bragging around the dinner table about our escapades.

As a grown man, it's easy to walk the same turf and just see a muddy creek, a pile of scrap lumber, and a few scraggly trees. The land hasn't changed — but I have. So often, I'm stressed, busy, and preoccupied with getting things done. Making ends meet. Keeping people happy.

How I long to re-connect with the wonder of discovery. To approach God's presence with the same sense of expectancy that sent me running across cornfields and clamoring through creek beds in pursuit of adventure.

Could it be that this is a key we've been missing in our spiritual journeys? It's easy to approach God like a stop at the gas station or a quick grocery run. But God is not a vending machine or a drive-through. He's not a menu to order from — he is a mystery to enter into, experience, and be changed by.

THE CRYSTAL CAVERN

Imagine yourself standing at the entrance of a giant cavern. Something deep within your heart calls you into its depths. As strange as it sounds, you feel like this cave has found you. You weren't looking for it, and yet here you stand at its mouth. Truth is, you have found yourself standing here many times before. But the more you avoid it, the stronger the draw becomes.

Suddenly, a faint whisper blows by in the wind, "Enter in."

This cave represents the depths of intimacy with God. Maybe you are frozen with fear or at a standstill because of laziness or apathy. Regardless, as long as you remain at the mouth of the cave, you'll be a powerless Christian. But don't worry, you won't be alone. In fact, you'll be in good company with the vast majority of American churchgoers. Good, moral, tolerant people. Folks with a nice family, nice career, and nice life.

However, if you long to explore the depths of God — if you long to become a dangerous Christian — a terrifyingly wonderful adventure awaits. You decide to explore further, leaving the comfort of the crowd, and your heart rate picks up with each glimmering rock face that your eyes notice. The beauty in front of you beckons you deeper, yet you can't shake a sense of angst, as if you are about to be exposed.

The path becomes narrower, steeper. You find yourself ducking to fit through the narrow passageway. The condition of your heart begins to flash before you, and the intensity and rawness of those images bring you to your knees. Searing pain courses through your body as the depths of your wayward heart come into full view. Everything that you have hidden, covered up, and denied throughout your life is made visible…and it seems too much to bear.

At this point, most people turn back, retreating to the safety of all they know and can control. For those who forge on, the tunnel becomes even more narrow and treacherous, pressing in on your body and robbing your lungs of air. In sheer desperation, you muster the little strength you have left to claw yourself along the narrow path.

The rock walls scrape at your flesh on every side. Never before have you experienced the literal weight of sin in your life. The floodgates open within you. Remorse, guilt, and shame pour out, as if your soul itself is weeping. If you had known this gut-wrenching anguish awaited, you never would have entered the cave. Yet, in the midst of this utter brokenness, a still, quiet voice urges you to press on.

Just as hopelessness strangles your last breath, the tunnel opens up into a gigantic crystal room. Standing to your feet, fresh breath fills your lungs as your eyes take in the magnificent beauty. Looking down, you expect to see exposed flesh and blood. Instead, your eyes fall on clean, healthy skin. All of the guilt, shame, and filth were left behind in the tunnel.

Freedom. Relieved and refreshed, you are captivated by wonder on every side. Enormous crystals as clear as diamonds stand like redwoods as far as you can see. A small pathway weaves throughout the crystal forest, each bend revealing formations more breathtaking than the last. A deep red hue of light illuminates each of the towering crystals. The deeper you move, the brighter the mysterious light grows.

A wave of thirst overtakes your body as your eyes fall on a deep pool of water, light emanating from its depths. Everything in you desires to plunge in, but you pause uncertainly, noticing footprints leading up to the pool. Others once stood in your very position, but the majority of them turned from the pool and walked away.

You hear a whisper: "Die to yourself." Startled, you look around for a source of the voice…nothing. What could this mean? Surely you weren't brought all this way to die. Yet, this is the same voice that beckoned you into the cavern, encouraged you to press on through the narrow tunnel, and brought you to this breathtakingly beautiful place.

Against all logic, you dive into the pool, swimming frantically toward the light. Your lungs burn with lack of oxygen. Your body gasps for air, but there is none to be found. Everything goes black, and your limp body sinks to the bottom of the pool.

Warmth. Warmth soothes your lungs, your heart, and your chest. Warmth moves down your arms and into your legs. The warmth of the deep red light envelops your body. It is love — pure, overwhelming, life-changing, indescribable love — and you find yourself weeping.

Then a whisper. "You died to yourself; now you can experience my love. Have I not promised you? You will seek me and find me when you seek me with all your heart."

There is no end to the crystal cavern — to the depths of intimacy with God. Adventure, mystery, and wonder await those committed and brave enough to spend a lifetime exploring its depths. This journey will transform you, but there is a price to pay.

THE COST OF SEEKING

The Hebrew word for "seek" — *darash* — literally means to tread or frequent, to follow, pursue, and diligently search for.[1] Many of us start out our spiritual journeys with passion and excitement, but shrink back from seeking God when we realize it will cost us our comfort, safety, and ultimately our self-constructed identity. The deeper we move into God's presence, the more we become aware of our depravity, failures, pride, and stubbornness.

In such moments, we are faced with a pivotal question: do we want to become more like Christ and experience him, or do we want to enjoy the delusion of comfort? Satan wants us to view the crystal caverns of God's presence as a prison that keeps us from the good life, rather than the only true pathway to the fullness of joy and eternal pleasures (PS. 16:11).

Save yourself, he whispers. *How could a good God let you hurt like this? Would a loving father really ask so much?*

Pursuing God requires vulnerability. This journey of dying to ourselves removes every mask and exposes every facade and false motive. We can't fake it with the God of the Universe! "Nothing in all creation is hidden from God's sight. Everything is uncovered and laid bare before the eyes of him to whom we must give account" (HEB. 4:13).

I have a friend and mentor who always says, "Reality is an acquired taste." Living in reality can sometimes be painful. The more we experience God's beauty, holiness, and goodness, the more we see parts of ourselves that we'd rather hide or minimize—willful sin, inadequacies, mistakes, and failures. We are undone in the presence of God, like Isaiah, who cried out, "Woe to me…I am ruined! For I am a man of unclean lips, and I live among a people of unclean lips, and my eyes have seen the King, the LORD Almighty" (IS. 6:5).

Our culture places a strong emphasis on feeling good, but I guarantee you, Isaiah wasn't jumping up and down in excitement here. He was face down on the floor, overwhelmed by God's holiness and his own impure heart. Yet this gut-wrenching experience of humility is a necessary and critical aspect of our seeking, because in it, we discover a God who sees all of our mess and imperfections and yet invites us to come exactly as we are.

In Hannah Hurnard's allegory, *Hinds' Feet on High Places,* Much Afraid reminds us of a mind-bending truth about God: "His kingly grace is lavished on my need and worthlessness. My blemishes he will not see but loves the beauty that shall be."[2] . Because of Jesus' sacrifice on the cross, God's hatred for sin is ultimately overshadowed by his love and desire to redeem. He sees our true selves—the men and women he longs to shape us into—and reaches out to welcome and heal us with wide-open arms.

Paul admonishes us to continually work out our salvation with fear and trembling (PHIL. 2:12), suggesting that this isn't a one-time experience, but a lifelong journey. It's like a master swordsmith who thrusts a hunk of iron into the furnace until the metal is red hot and malleable. The craftsman then takes a maul and beats the iron into the desired shape, plunging it into a bucket of water to wash away any impurities. The swordsmith will repeat this process again and again until he can hold the sword up in front of him and see his own reflection.

And so it is with our sanctification, if we choose to press through moments of conviction, leaning into grace. To be transformed by God, we must first be exposed. While the journey will not be painless, the end result is always breathtaking. "Taste and see that the Lord is good," the psalmist reflects (PS. 34:8). The Hebrew word for "good"—*towb*—means beautiful, and it is the beauty and holiness of God's presence that obliterates sin.[3] No longer are we in bondage to what other people think—we know *whose* we are. Our primary aim isn't getting ahead or being successful in the world's eyes; it's walking in tune with the Holy Spirit and being used by him.

This spiritual journey is beautifully described in *The Last Battle,* C.S. Lewis's final book in *The Chronicles of Narnia* series. "I have come home at last!" Jewel the unicorn exclaims. "This is my real country! I belong here. This is the land I have been looking for all my life, though I never knew it till now." Inviting Peter, Lucy, and Edmund beyond the borders of all they have known or experienced in Narnia, Jewel beckons. "Come further up, come further in!"[4] Similarly, the Holy Spirit invites you and I into the depths of God. This journey will not always be easy, but it will be worth it. If we dare to press in to God through tight spaces and painful moments, we will live into God's grace and our belovedness.

SEARCHING FOR HOME

If you've ever seen the movie *August Rush,* you know the story of eleven-year-old Evan Taylor. Evan risks everything to leave his orphanage, the only home he has known, in hopes of finding his mother and father. He is determined to go to any length to connect with his parents.[5]

In one way or another, we can all relate to this orphan longing. The emotional grip of yearning for our true home is hard to shake. We were designed for intimacy with our Heavenly Father, and God often uses this ache to draw us back to himself. For Evan, seeking out and finding his mother and father wasn't just a nice idea or something he should do — it was something he *couldn't not* do. Similarly, our pursuit of God cannot be sustained by obligation or guilt trips. **Seeking is fueled, driven, and motivated by desire**.

Scripture admonishes us to cling to the things that we have heard "lest we drift away" (HEB. 2:1). The Greek context here refers to mooring a ship — using chains or ropes to attach a boat to a wharf, buoy, or anchor so it is not pulled out to sea by ocean currents and changing winds.[6] Apart from Christ, we will be tossed about by the waves of life and longing. Longing for something — anything — that promises to satisfy us. It's how I spent much of my twenties, and it never delivers. True soul rest comes only when we moor ourselves in the safe harbor of Christ, and there find our true home. Even in the seeking, there is security and safety.

David wrestled with this in real time. Hiding in the wilderness as Saul was trying to kill him, he cried out, "You, God, are my God, earnestly I seek you; I thirst for you, my whole being longs for you, in a dry and parched land where there is no water" (PS. 63:1).

"One thing I have asked from the LORD," he further testifies, "that I shall seek: that I may dwell in the house of the LORD all the days of my life, to behold the beauty of the LORD and to meditate in his temple" (PS. 27:4, NASB). Oh that this would be the cry of our hearts!

In the Old Testament, God's presence resided in the tabernacle. In order to commune with God, King David had to roll out of bed, put on his robe, head across town to the tabernacle, and go through an extensive cleansing process (see EX. 30) before being able to enter the tabernacle and worship. With this cultural context in mind, Paul's words to New Testament believers are truly earth-shattering: "Do you not know that you are God's temple and that God's Spirit dwells in you?" (1 COR. 3:16, ESV).

What? God dwelling in you and me? The idea would have been provocative and hard to comprehend for first-century Jews, who since their childhood had traveled the long, dusty roads of Palestine to reach the temple. Because of Jesus, you and I have a direct access to the presence of God—at any moment. No traversing the countryside or physically washing our bodies. No buying animals for a sacrifice or waiting for a priest to approach God on our behalf.

All he asks is that we come, quiet our hearts, and tune in with his Spirit. We are already clean through the shed blood of Jesus, and he is our High Priest. He has brought God to us!

Building intimacy with God takes effort, practice, and intentionality. But not in the way you might expect: " '[N]o eye has seen, nor ear heard, nor the heart of man imagined, what God has prepared for those who love him'—these things God has revealed to us through the Spirit. For the Spirit searches everything, even the depths of God" (1 COR. 2:9-10, ESV).

We will spend all of eternity exploring God, discovering beauty and delights and facets of his character that we cannot even imagine—far beyond the grandeur of a crystal cavern. But it's not just one day, it's today, through the power of the Holy Spirit. He is our divine guide, navigating the twists and turns of life and giving us wisdom, insight and knowledge as we crawl deeper into the mystery of God. There is no limit to how much we can know Jesus—we can go as far as we are willing to pursue him.

Theologians and contemplatives throughout history challenge our modern-day categories of secular and sacred, offering a rich spiritual heritage of disciplines and practices to stir up our affections for Jesus beyond what we have come to call "quiet times." Brother Lawrence suggests that every moment is an opportunity to experience God and know him more:

> We must know before we can love. In order to know God, we must often think of him; and when we come to love him, we shall then also think of him often, for our heart will be with our treasure . . . we need only to recognize God intimately present with us, to address ourselves to him every moment.[7]

How would it change our day-to-day faith walk if we truly grasped that all of life is infused with God? My introduction to this reality began in the pages of *Celebration of Discipline*. (I encourage you to read this book if you haven't!) Richard Foster discusses a number of creative ways to connect with God in addition to Bible study, prayer, and worship.[8]

Growing closer to Jesus might look like getting on your knees or taking a walk in the woods. Journaling, listening to music, or engaging your senses with the truths of who God is at your emotional core. Letting God restore your soul in solitude as you rest and soak in silence, or gathering with fellow Christians to share a meal and your hearts. Celebrating God's blessings in community, or weeping in each other's arms as you bear the weight of suffering.

The promise of seeking God is not health, wealth, or an easy life. It is meaning, purpose—his presence with us—that opens us up to experience spiritual abundance, even in the midst of suffering. This makes us incredibly dangerous. Satan can no longer cripple us with temptation or difficulty, for even hardship can become fuel to deeper intimacy with God.

CULTIVATING SPIRITUAL HUNGER

"My soul thirsts for God, for the living God. When can I go and meet with God?" (ps. 42:2). Satan does everything in his power to distract us and numb our spiritual senses—to make us desire anyone and anything rather than crying out to God like David did. Recognizing this invisible battle for desire is critical for our spiritual growth.

I wonder, what in your life stirs up your hunger and thirst for God? And what dulls and numbs it? For me, my phone, Facebook, even ESPN can become a source of preoccupation. These things, though not bad in and of themselves, can easily make me zone out and forget the greatness and wonder and depths of God at my fingertips.

In ancient times, the Israelites often slept on the flat roofs of their homes. The last thing they saw at night was the grandeur of the starlit sky, and each morning, they awoke to the rising sun in all its glory. Daily rhythms like this serve an important purpose in our spiritual lives. They remind our hearts of who God is and all that he is for us and in us.

What about you? What calibrates your mind and heart for the day? How easy it is to let the world invade with all its worries, cares, and stresses. We can check Facebook, review our calendars, and get a jump-start on e-mails before even getting out of bed. We barrel through the day at breakneck speed—stressed, worried, and anxious. But, oh the joys we miss out on!

In the Gospels, Jesus tells the story of "a merchant looking for fine pearls" (MT. 13:45). Pearls were among the most expensive and exquisite jewelry during the Roman Empire. The Roman general Vitellius is said to have funded an entire military campaign by selling one of his mother's pearl earrings, and Pliny writes that two pearls were worth 1,875,000 ounces of silver. That's over nine million dollars' worth![9]

When Jesus spoke of pearls, he was referring to far more than an ordinary bauble.

One day, the merchant's entire world turned upside down when he discovered *the* pearl. We're not told what made it stand out, but one thing is clear: it was very precious and of inestimable worth. Everything else paled in comparison.

Only this one thing mattered. So much so that the man went and sold every last thing he owned in order to make the pearl his own. What do you value more than anything? Is it your status, your career, even your family or ministry? You and I are Jesus' pearl of great price. Often, we may not feel worthy or worth it, but Jesus values us above everything else in all creation. So much so that he gave up everything—even his own life—to make us his own treasured possession.

In our humanity, we're prone to forget the true spiritual reality that is ours as the precious sons and daughters of God. Spiritual amnesia is in our DNA. Solitude, rest, celebration, mediation, community—these are tangible, day-to-day ways of re-connecting with our true identity. Building these practices into our lives, not as legalistic performances, but as sustainable spiritual rhythms, opens wide our hearts to know God and ourselves in a deeper way.

Whatever you may cling to for worth, identity or safety, let me tell you, Jesus is better. "Oh, the depth of the riches of the wisdom and knowledge of God! How unsearchable his judgments, and his paths beyond tracing out!" (ROM. 11:33-34). "Who has known the mind of the Lord?" the passage continues. And our answer resounds, *we have!* Through Jesus, we are in God and he is in us. But it came at a tremendous price, a price Satan wants us to forget.

What keeps you from engaging with the Spirit of God? Are you willing to let it go? I encourage you, be ruthless in your pursuit of the Pearl of Greatest Price. Turn off, get rid of, and say "no" to whatever you have to in order to stay hungry and thirsty. You won't regret it!

AN INVITATION TO ABUNDANCE

God stopped at nothing to pursue you. Like a special ops paratrooper behind enemy lines, he stormed the gates of hell to take back our rightful identity as sons and daughters of God. We don't have to earn or perform our way back—in fact, we never could.

But like Peter, we've all denied Jesus (JN. 18:13-27). Not just once, but multiple times. With our words and our actions, our decisions and priorities. Whenever we forge ahead in our own strength rather than seeking his face, our lives utter the words, "I don't know him."

Peter uttered those words over a charcoal fire. As he tried to warm his hands, his heart was cold and hard. Is it any wonder, then, that when Jesus rose from the dead, he sought out Peter, making him breakfast over—you guessed it—a charcoal fire?

"Come and have breakfast," he invited the estranged, doubting disciples (JN. 21:12). There, Jesus fully restored Peter. Thousands of years later, his invitation rings true here and now.

"Come and eat, my beloved," he beckons us. "Come, taste of my riches. Drink of the delights of my presence. Gorge your hungry soul on my love for you."

"Come, all you who are thirsty, come to the waters; and you who have no money, come, buy and eat! Come, buy wine and milk without money and without cost. Why spend money on what is not bread, and your labor on what does not satisfy? Listen, listen to me, and eat what is good, and your soul will delight in the richest of fare" (IS. 55:2).

Despite every way we have betrayed or forgotten him, Jesus invites us to the charcoal fire—offering not just breakfast, but reconciliation, redemption, and abundance. What is the most rich, lavish thing you can imagine? Multiply that by a million! In Jesus, we have access to all the blessings of God (2 COR. 1:20).

I've never been to the Great Barrier Reef but I hope to, some day. It's teeming with life—fish, dolphins, sharks, seahorses, coral and animals that scientists haven't even discovered yet. Sail across the smooth waters of the Reef, and you might see a fish or two, perhaps a dolphin, but you'll miss out on the wonder. It's hidden below the surface—in the depths.

We will spend all of eternity discovering God—he is endless. So if you think you know God, your God is too small. I beg you, don't miss out on the opportunity to dive deep into the Great Barrier Reef of God's love and see for yourself "how wide and long and high and deep is the love of Christ, and to know this love that surpasses knowledge—that you may be filled to the measure of all the fullness of God" (EPH. 3:17-19).

The beauty and mystery of the Christian life is that Jesus doesn't just send us out to work for him. He invites us out of ourselves. He cooks us breakfast. He redeems. He nourishes our souls. All we need do is come to him, with the same intensity that Peter abandoned everything to jump in the water and swim to Jesus. The only thing that will fuel that kind of pursuit is knowing, deep in the core of our souls, that he is good. That we can trust him. That we can never out sin him. That he'll always take us back—again and again and again.

Sometimes it's hard to rest in God's love and compassion—to really believe it is true. Our relationships with our earthly parents strongly influence how we see our Heavenly Father. I have an awesome loving Dad, but even so, God has used my wife Ashley to give me a more healthy and complete perspective of himself. One day, as we sat on a bluff overlooking Table Rock Lake, I asked Ashley how she imagined God when she worshipped him.

"I picture myself crawling up into my Daddy's lap." Her answer surprised me.

When I came before God, I often envisioned quite a different scene: Jesus seated on his throne, at the right hand of God the Father, surrounded by twenty-four elders on their faces worshipping him. I tend to approach God reflecting on his power, authority, justice, and might, but Ashley reminded me that God is also tender, compassionate, merciful, and forgiving.

Both of these perspectives are true, but limited. That's why we need brothers and sisters in Christ along the journey of seeking God. Satan will go to any length to isolate you from other believers so he can whisper lies into your head. Don't let him. **Becoming a dangerous Christian isn't just something you do in your prayer closet — it also happens in community**. I encourage you to grab a few companions for the journey, and dare to enter the crystal cavern together.

Seeking God is ultimately about saying "yes." Not shrinking back in fear, but taking risks to step out in faith. Believing that even when it means dying to our plans and dreams, we can trust the good and beautiful that he has just around the corner.

So look for God at every turn. Listen for him — as "a still small voice" (I KI. 19:12), in "the roar of rushing waters" (EZEK. 43:2), and any other way he might choose to speak. When we chase after him with all our hearts, it's not about getting a certain answer or getting our way.

There is sheer delight in hearing his voice…and being changed.

CHAPTER SIX

HEARING GOD

God invites us to look up, open our eyes to the wonder all around us, and seize every opportunity to encounter him.
—*Margaret Feinberg*

LIVING IN LA, I SPENT MANY AN AFTERNOON CATCHING WAVES, trying desperately to ward off the emptiness I felt. Like many things in my life at the time, surfing was all about the thrill, the high, the intensity. Sadly, I rarely hit the beach sober.

I lived for the moments when I popped up effortlessly and rode the curl of a perfect wave. Speeding along with the wind in my face, I felt alive, free, and a bit superhuman. My insecurity and self-doubt melted away, and secretly, I hoped everyone else saw how awesome I looked.

But even the best wave is gone too soon. My few seconds of fame usually ended with a less-than-graceful fall and the burn of salt water up my nose. Emerging from the waves, I pushed my board through the swells again—hungry for another ride, desperate for a brief escape.

I hated that part—waiting. Restlessness drove my impatience. But no matter how many waves I caught, I couldn't escape that aching feeling of wanting more. I felt numb inside, as if all the excitement and thrill drained out of me and left me emptier than ever.

As I got to know Jesus and began to be discipled into a relationship with him, something changed. Not in an instant or overnight, but I felt a distinct shift. Paddling out past the breakers one day, I remember stopping just to sit there and take it all in—dolphins playing just a few yards away. Jellyfish swimming in tandem below. The warmth of the sun on my back. The distant roar of waves crashing on the shore. The smell of salt water in the air.

Joy and wonder welled up deep within me. *Wow, how did I not see this before?* I felt like a kid on Christmas morning as I reflected on all the good gifts God had surrounded me with, gifts I'd been completely blind to. The ocean hadn't changed—I was changing.

No need to impress others or be the best surfer on the beach (fortunate for me, because I was far from it!). None of that mattered anymore as I experienced the truth of Zephaniah 3:17: "The LORD your God is with you, the Mighty Warrior who saves. He will take great delight in you; in his love he will no longer rebuke you, but will rejoice over you with singing."

He delights in me. Hearing God in the echoes of the seagulls flying overhead and sensing his presence in the breathtaking beauty of the coastline, I was undone. Without uttering a single word, Jesus spoke to my heart in a real and powerful way. All of it a testament to his love, an undeserved gift of his grace.

All this—for me? The warm sunshine, the perfect waves, the clear blue sky...even the strength in my legs to be able to pop up and take on each new wave. In that moment, everything was clear. I didn't need to be affirmed or noticed or have my moment of fame. I was *seen* and known and celebrated, awestruck at the beauty that revealed God's pursuit of my wayward heart.

I wonder...how often do we miss God speaking to us? Maybe we're numb, distracted, too busy, or seeking momentary thrills. How can we open our hearts to hear, see, and experience the abundant life he came to bring us? Grab your board and let's surf it out.

MORE THAN A DIVINE TEXT MESSAGE

Texting is great. It's convenient, easy, and it helps us stay more connected—at least on a surface level—than ever before. I can carry on multiple conversations simultaneously with friends across the country—even across the world. Gone are the days of waiting for letters to arrive in the mail or paying for long-distance phone calls.

Pew Research reports that almost one in three Americans prefer texting to phone conversations; a similar survey estimates that 52% of consumers favor texting over talking.[1] Teenagers lead the way with an average of 110 messages a day — over 3,200 a month — have you seen how fast their fingers can move?![2] Yet for all the conveniences of texting, there are some pitfalls. It's easy to misread or miss contextual information, even with emojis to try and fill in the gaps!

Communication is fundamentally a relational experience between two people. Did you know that up to 90% of communication is non-verbal? One researcher estimates that, when someone is talking about their feelings or attitudes, 55% of the communication is conveyed through body language, 38% through tone of voice, and a mere 7% through the actual words spoken.[3] Wow! There's a lot we can lose when we reduce our relationships to a texting exchange or words on a page. Any conversation will be incomplete if we rely too heavily on one form of communication at the exclusion of others.

The same is true with us and God. "Hearing God" is common Christian-speak, but what does it actually look like? It's easy to over-spiritualize this, forgetting that God is well acquainted with our humanity. After all, he invented each one of our senses and his image echoes within our natural curiosities. Let's unpack it together and take a look at some common ways God communicates with us through his Spirit:

God's Word. John Piper hit the nail on the head when he said, "If you want to hear the voice of God, read from this book out loud," holding up his Bible.[4] Miraculously, God put words on paper through divine inspiration to give us the foundation of our faith and knowledge of him. One of the beauties of Scripture is the immediate accessibility of God's voice through it, as the Holy Spirit reveals God's truth through its pages.

So, if I think that God is talking to me and it doesn't line up with the Word, it most certainly isn't God's voice. A dangerous Christian holds the Sword of the Spirit in high regard as our number one source of hearing from God. However, in our well-meaning desire to be true to the Scripture, we can be guilty of trying to put the Creator of the Universe in a box, forgetting that he can speak however he wants.

God's creation. Every painting has an artist, every sculpture has a sculptor, and every creation has a creator. All God has made bears witness to who he is. "Since the creation of the world, God's invisible qualities—his eternal power and divine nature—have been clearly seen, being understood from what has been made" (ROM. 1:20). Without speaking a single word, each mountain peak, rushing river, and blazing sunset boldly declares the truth about God (PS. 19:1).

I love surfing and hunting—mainly because I get to be alone in God's creation. Being surrounded by God's beauty and grandeur literally restores my soul. It reminds me of who God is and, no matter what stresses or hardships I'm facing, that he is sovereign and present. Being a dad teaches me a whole lot about God, too. It's mind-blowing, really—watching each of our kids' personalities begin to develop and blossom. And to see that every child is different and unique, beautiful and hilarious. As Ashley and I parent, we get to be witnesses of who God is through observing his creative work in each of our children.

Christian community. The Holy Spirit dwells in fellow believers, and God often uses them as mouthpieces in our lives. One of the golden threads that runs through the book of Proverbs is wise counsel: "Where there is strife, there is pride, but wisdom is found in those who take advice" (PROV. 13:10). How many times has someone encouraged you in your faith? How many times has a friend spoken just the right words at the right time? That was the God of the Universe choosing to speak into your life through one of his children.

"Community" is a buzzword in Christian circles these days, but it's not always easy to live out. When David was hiding his adultery, God sent Nathan to confront him and speak truth into his life (2 SAM. 12:7). In moments like this, our true self comes out. Will we respond in repentance or buck up against God's voice? Are we willing to be humble enough to listen, or bold enough to allow God to speak through us? This feels dangerous, and runs completely counter to everything American culture is about—pride, independence, and self-sufficiency.

Dreams and visions. "I will pour out my Spirit on all people," God promises. "Your sons and daughters will prophesy, your old men will dream dreams, your young men will see visions" (JOEL 2:28). This one can weird us out a bit as western Christians. Camp directors from all over the world come to Kanakuk to be trained, and I'm always fascinated to learn about God at work in their cultures. I've heard many a story of Jesus revealing himself in dreams—in places where evangelism is illegal and Bibles aren't available, God is not limited.

In my own life, I was really struggling to forgive a friend and my heart was hard. Then one night, I had a dream. I was walking through a peaceful park when this friend showed up. He started walking toward me and tried to give me a hug, but I pushed him away. He threw his arms around me, and I found myself hugging him back. Something snapped. We held each other and began weeping so hard that we fell to the ground. I woke up and that same forgiveness that washed over me in my dream washed over me in reality. I had tried for months to forgive, but now all of the sudden, I was finally free.

We have to be careful to interpret dreams and visions, along with everything else, in light of God's Word. In my case, I realized this was not a word of Satan—he hates forgiveness and would want me to rot in bitterness and anger. This was not a work of my flesh—I'm not strong enough to muster up that kind of compassion. I had tried and failed. The only other option was God. It was his power, not mine, that worked forgiveness in my heart.

Any way he wants. In Scripture, we read accounts of God speaking through burning bushes and sheepskins. Thunderstorms. Plagues. Rainbows. He's communicated through angels and prophets, pillars of fire and even donkeys. Talk about creative! God speaks in a million different ways, but perhaps we miss out because we are looking for a divine text message—for handwriting on the wall or an audible voice booming from the sky.

The more we are attuned to these various ways God reveals himself, the more our relationship with him will blossom. God is not just a hope to believe in, but a mystery to be sought, and the delights of salvation aren't just for heaven. Jesus said, "This is eternal life, that they may know you, the only true God, and Jesus Christ whom you have sent" (JN. 17:3). When we catch a glimpse of the riches available to us, we will stop at nothing to know him more. And dwelling in Christ makes us spiritually dangerous. When we have nothing to lose and nothing to prove, we are emboldened to stand up against evil and speak life and hope.

SEEING WITH NEW EYES

Could it be, then, that experiencing God isn't only about forging into new territory, but also seeing what we've become blind to... and hearing what we've too long dismissed? God's Word promises, "Then will the eyes of the blind be opened and the ears of the deaf unstopped. Then will the lame leap like a deer and the mute tongue shout for joy" (IS. 35:5-6). We tend to think of spiritual maturity as becoming dignified and knowledgeable, using big theological words and getting our "act" together. But this passage is all about discovery and freedom.

Even the mild winters of Southern Missouri can be rather torturous, especially with five kids running circles in our three-bedroom house. As soon as spring hits, Ashley and I always take the kids out to Lake Taneycomo. Inevitably, they end up soaked head to toe and covered with mud, their teeth chattering from the frigid waters. But none of that hinders them from roughhousing in the grass, chasing geese, and digging for snails along the rocky shore.

There's not one iota of obligation in the way my kids approach the world. Just pure, unhindered delight. Every day, every moment is a new opportunity to learn and grow and experience. Perhaps this is why Jesus so clearly said, "Unless you change and become like little children, you will never enter the kingdom of heaven" (MT. 18:3).

Belle discovered the high dive when she was three. I remember watching in astonishment as she climbed the ladder and walked to the edge of her own initiative. Wide open and fearless, she leapt out over the pool. There wasn't a doubt in her mind that

Daddy would be there to catch her in the water. For Knox, every imaginary scenario he dreams up ends in a wrestling match. As I toss him across the room and onto the couch, he giggles, "Do it again! Do it again!" I can't help but see in his face the very passion with which I long to come to Jesus.

Just beyond the commitments, stresses, and worries that crowd our minds lies uncharted territory—God present, engaged, and at work all around us. But somewhere along the way of "growing up," it's easy to lose our sense of childlike wonder. To forget that this life of faith is the most exhilarating experience in the entire world.

"Having eyes do you not see?" Jesus lovingly beckons. "[A]nd having ears do you not hear?" (MK. 8:18, ESV) Sin has dulled our spiritual senses, and in one way or another, we can all find ourselves in the stories of Bartimaeus (MK. 10) and the man from Bethsaida (MK. 8).

"What do you want me to do for you?" Jesus asks Bartimaeus—and us.

No fancy words or theological treatises, just the cry of our desperate hearts: "I want to see" (MK. 10:51). Jesus spits on the blind man's eyes, his own saliva a testament to the humanness of God-with-us. And then, something miraculous happens.

The man from Bethsaida begins to see, but it's all blurry. He can make out vague moving shapes—people, like trees walking around (MK. 8:23). I don't know about you, but I've had my share of blurry moments spiritually, where things look jumbled up, messy, and confusing.

Thankfully, all is not lost. Jesus lays his hands on the man's eyes, restoring his vision completely. Can you imagine seeing for the first time in your life, glimpsing the true reality of who God is and who you are? *That* is the promise that fuels our seeking.

Living dangerously is not ultimately about going after Satan with a vengeance. It's about seeing and savoring Jesus. "I pray that the eyes of your heart may be enlightened..." Paul writes in Ephesians (1:18). When we catch glimpses of who he is—when we live in childlike wonder—everything else begins to make sense. Pursuing Christ isn't about white-knuckling it, trying harder, or doing more to get in "good" with God. Instead, it's an invitation to approach each day listening for God and looking for him in the most ordinary of places.

YOU NEED A FILTER

How do you know if it's God speaking? It's a critical question to wrestle with as we seek to discern God's voice. Scripture exhorts us, "[T]est everything that is said. Hold on to what is good. Stay away from every kind of evil" (1 THESS. 5:21-22, NLT). One of our programs at Kanakuk is a survival camp, where kids explore the Ozark Mountains for two weeks. They'll tell you that in any survival situation, finding water is a top priority.

But not just any water. It's never a good idea to drink from a stagnant pond, and even when the water is flowing freely, it's important to ask, *where's the source? Where is it coming from?* Even a pristine creek, bubbling down the mountainside, may not be safe if the water is contaminated by animal carcasses or waste upstream. Unless you find yourself at the water source—here in the Ozarks we have springs that bubble straight out of the rock—it's always a good idea to filter water before drinking it.

Sure, it's an extra step, and you might be really thirsty, but putting in the extra effort to pump water through a carbon filter will ensure that any sediment, bacteria, and viruses in the water never make it into your body. The filter catches all the bad stuff, and you're left with a clear, pure glass of water. Filtered water will satiate your thirst in the moment, and it's good for you, too—it won't wreak havoc in your body or come back to haunt you.

Blindly accepting whatever idea pops into your head, whatever song comes on the radio, or whatever someone else says as God speaking to you is like gulping down the first water you discover without stopping to think—playing into Satan's schemes to make you spiritually sick. But we also fall prey to the devil when we dismiss these real-world experiences completely, assuming that God can only speak to us through the pages of the Bible. Even in our reading of Scripture, we err when we proof text, picking a

verse out of its context and claiming it for ourselves while failing
to deeply read and understand God's heart.

The devil will do anything in his power to minimize the reality
of God's voice. If he can't make you deny God's existence, he'll
try to numb your spiritual senses by discounting even one of the
ways that God speaks. Fall for it, and your perception of God will
be significantly limited. Some of us place too much emphasis on
personal experience and fail to apply ourselves to the Word of
God, while others of us cling to a very small view of God as only
revealing himself in Scripture, neglecting the multi-faceted ways
he longs to communicate with us.

Whichever side you tend to drift toward, the solution is the
same: **you need a filter in order to be spiritually healthy and
flourish in your relationship with God**. That filter is the Holy
Spirit working in tandem with the Word of God, much like a
carbon filter includes both a sediment screen and a charcoal core.
George Müller reminds us of "the all-sufficiency of the Holy
Scriptures as our rule, and the Holy Spirit as our teacher."[5] The
two go hand in hand.

No wonder Satan works so hard to create conflict about the
place of God's Word versus the Holy Spirit! Their collaborative
work reveals the true voice of God. This is not just a theological
truth, but a daily reality we have access to, if we seek it out.

But it hasn't always been so. When God revealed himself at
Mount Sinai, the Israelites cried out to Moses (DEUT. 5:24-25):

> *"This great fire will consume us, and we will die if we hear
> the voice of the Lord our God any longer. For what mortal
> has ever heard the voice of the living God speaking out of
> fire, as we have, and survived? Go near and listen to all that
> the Lord our God says. Then tell us whatever the Lord our
> God tells you. We will listen and obey."*

God's voice was so overwhelming that the Israelites were afraid
for their lives! Throughout the Old Testament we see countless
examples of God speaking, most often to prophets and spiritual
leaders. The phrase "The word of the Lord came to…" actually
shows up in the Bible 128 times.

Here are a few examples (1 KI. 17:2-4; JER. 1:4-5):

> *The word of the Lord came to Elijah: "Leave here, turn eastward and hide in the Kerith Ravine, east of the Jordan. You will drink from the brook, and I have directed the ravens to supply you with food there."*
>
> *The word of the Lord came to [Jeremiah], saying, "Before I formed you in the womb I knew you, before you were born I set you apart; I appointed you as a prophet to the nations."*

The Bible doesn't tell us exactly what each of these situations looked like. Did these guys hear a booming voice from heaven or a quiet whisper? Did God come to them in some kind of human form or did they experience a gut knowing of his words in their hearts?

What we do know is that the God of the Universe communicated in such a way that people could understand and respond. They knew it was God speaking, not the lentils they'd had for lunch. And God does not change—which means he is still speaking today in just as real and tangible ways.

LEARNING TO LISTEN

"Long ago, at many times and in many ways, God spoke to our fathers by the prophets, but in these last days he has spoken to us by his Son" (HEB. 1:1-2, ESV). When Jesus gave up his spirit on Calvary, the curtain in front of the Holy of Holies was torn from top to bottom, giving us complete access to intimacy with God. Because of Jesus, God doesn't just speak to the super-spiritual or a few chosen individuals who are "worthy." He speaks to all of us, if we quiet our hearts to listen and humble ourselves to come into his presence.

And how often does he speak? I love asking our campers about this and watching their brain wheels turn. Maybe once, when we accept Christ? Or when we have big decisions to make, like what career to choose or who to marry? Maybe, too, when we're in a really rough spot and need him to protect and comfort us?

We think too small. Way too small. **The reality is that God is speaking to us all the time—every single moment of every**

single day! "For God speaks again and again, though people do not recognize it" (JOB 33:14, NLT). I pray that we will not be among those people. Over the last several years, I have become obsessed with the voice of God. Right now, no matter what is going on in your life, God is speaking over your heart. Here are some things to look for:

Revelation. It's a light bulb experience—a spiritual "aha" moment. You've probably had a time in your life when you felt confused or stuck, stumbling around in the dark trying to figure things out. Then, whether through prayer, a conversation with a friend, reading Scripture, time in his creation or some other context, it's as if God snaps his fingers and you get it—not just in your head, but in your heart. It's a deep gut knowing, a certainty about what is good and true and what matters. That's revelation from God—the real-time working of the Holy Spirit.

Illumination. Just as a dimmer switch controls the intensity of the light, brightening the room bit by bit, illumination often happens when we're reading God's Word. You may have read a Scripture a hundred times in your life and then all of the sudden, it's as if the Lord turns up the dimmer switch and the meaning of the text comes to life. He has illumined the text. That is the God of the Universe speaking into your life.

Conviction. For the majority of my life, I've hated the feeling of conviction. The pit in my stomach, the taste of shame in my mouth—yuck! However, in John 16:8, we discover that one of the roles of the Holy Spirit is to convict. Every time we feel convicted, that is God speaking to us. What a staggering thought! God cares enough to convict us in even the smallest details of life. Instead of being a grouch, we should be jumping up and down on the table, saying, "Thank you God for caring enough about me to speak into this situation!"

Prompting and nudging. This is when the Holy Spirit pushes, presses, or tugs at your heart. You may feel compelled to act, pulled out of your comfort zone, driven to do something that you otherwise wouldn't. It's easy to ignore this kind of thing…to write it off as crazy thoughts in your head, or to freeze in fear of saying or doing the wrong thing and looking dumb. Don't, I beg you. Say yes.

Take the risk. Step out and obey. Engage with the Holy Spirit and you just may experience the voice of God speaking through you.

This list is by no means exhaustive, but it provides a launching point. As we begin to understand how God speaks, our ears perk up. We start filtering everything through his Word and his Spirit, and a whole new world opens up — a world of experiencing God in the here and now. Along the way, we'll be faced with some dangerous choices:

Will we shut down conviction, ignore illumination, and focus on what we want?

Or will we engage, lean in, and bend our ear to listen?

"The voice of the Spirit of God is as gentle as a summer breeze," Oswald Chambers reflects, "so gentle that unless you are living in complete fellowship and oneness with God, you will not hear it. The sense of warning and restraint that the Spirit gives comes to us in the most amazingly gentle ways."[6] The world we live in is chaotic, loud, and fast-paced. It doesn't lend itself well to listening and waiting on God, but paradoxically, this single-minded pursuit is the source of our spiritual power.

GROWING UP IN CHRIST

Ever since our daughter Tess got her legs under her, Ashley and I have been struggling to keep up. Whatever's within reach — from cell phones to bowls of cereal, crayons to crumbs on the floor — is a fascinating new discovery. (And with three older siblings, there's always something bright and colorful lying around!) These days, Tess is into everything. She finds joy in digging through my pockets and relentlessly trying to pull my socks off. I want to approach God with the same passion and curiosity. To shed the *have to* and embrace the *get to.* This contagious joy of exploration and discovery makes Satan tremble.

Any parent knows that risk is an inherent part of learning to walk. Toddlers fall down. A lot! Scraped knees and boo-boos are a regular occurrence around our house. Learning to hear God's voice is no different. But we can take a step toward Jesus each day — even just a baby step — and trust that when we fall down and get bloody knees, his grace will be there to set us on our feet again. Too many of us are unwilling to step out in seeking God for fear of looking foolish. But we can't learn if we are too afraid to try.

I'm a night owl by nature, so when one of my mentors encouraged me to spend time with God in the morning, I was pretty skeptical. *What makes the morning more holy?* I wondered. *Can't I hear God just as well at night?* But because I respected Chancey and his walk with God, I agreed to challenge myself.

The clanging of the alarm clock shook me, and my gut instantly began to churn. All those years of mandatory workouts with the football team at six in the morning came flooding black. In that moment, my passionate desire was for my pillow.

"This is going to be brutal," I moaned. Rubbing the sleep out of my eyes, I willed my feet to hit the floor and take a wobbly step toward Jesus. To sit in his presence, quiet my heart, and listen. To soak up his beauty and align my heart with the true reality of who I was as his son.

Some days, it felt like duty. But as time went on, I began to groan less and desire more. There was no flash of light from heaven, but slowly and steadily, I began to develop a hunger to be with Jesus. My heart was stirred up with love and desire for him. Almost as if I was moving from Tess's unsteady toddle to Knox's energetic sprint. I was learning to hear the voice of God.

"[T]rain yourself to be godly," Paul admonishes us (1 TIM. 4:7). The burn of a workout isn't exactly my definition of sheer delight, but showing up to the gym consistently, whether I feel like it or not, makes me stronger. It enables me to move beyond a short sprint to longer distances. And that I can get excited about.

It's easy to turn seeking God into a performance. We may set our alarm clocks super early and see how many chapters of Scripture we can sprint through, but move so fast that we fail to hear the whisperings of the Holy Spirit. That's why, at the end of the day, the posture of our hearts matters most. While there are certainly practices and rhythms that can facilitate or hinder hearing God's voice, the living dangerously cannot be reduced to a list.

Through Jesus, we can reach out and "take hold of the eternal life to which [we] were called" (1 TIM. 6:12). We can clamor up on our wobbly spiritual feet, grab hold of the Spirit's hand, and go seeking. Hosea's words echo with a similar sense of urgency: "Let us know; let us press on to know the Lord" (HOS. 6:3). I don't know about you, but I don't want to miss one moment of what God has for me. Hearing God's voice is a daily, never-ending pursuit that may include leaving the comfort of our pillows early in the morning but certainly doesn't end there.

Looking. Listening. Stopping to notice. This is the heartbeat of the spiritual life. "To fall in love with God is the greatest romance," Saint Augustine reflects, "to seek him, the greatest adventure; to find him, the greatest human achievement."[7] All we need do is come—humble, open, desperate for God's healing touch to quicken our spiritual senses. Because we've caught sight of the one thing that really matters and our eyes are riveted.

When we enter heaven's gates, may we be able to say with Paul, "I have fought the good fight, I have finished the race, I have kept the faith" (2 TIM. 4:7). Along the way, we'll need patience to slow down, rest, and listen for God's voice, as well as fierce tenacity to push through boredom, distraction, and temptation that Satan lobs our way.

As we grow in our spiritual awareness, we become an increasing threat to Satan's schemes. **The man or woman consumed with the voice of God is a dangerous Christian, and prayer is the pathway by which we access this power.** Let's explore together how we can reclaim this spiritual practice from the land of obligatory mealtime grace.

But first, what is God speaking over your heart? Pause, for just a moment, and listen.

DANGEROUS

PRAYER

CHAPTER SEVEN

THE WEAPON OF PRAYER

The essence of prayer does not consist in asking God for something, but in opening our hearts to God, in speaking with him, and living with him in perpetual communion.
—Sadhu Sundar Singh

"WHAT HAVE I GOTTEN MYSELF INTO?" I stood on the beach, my heart beating out of my chest as I waited for the starting pistol to fire. But it was not anticipation that spiked my heart rate.

It was fear. Doubt. Inner angst that tied my stomach up in knots and made me want to puke. As I stared this monster of a triathlon in the face, I was pretty sure it would consume me.

Chew me up and spit me out. I'll be honest, I'm not the best swimmer. You can ask my wife Ashley—she lovingly compares my swimming to that of a water buffalo!

This is going to be horrible. Why is no one else freaking out right now? Note to self, never sign up for another one of these again.

My soundtrack of doubt was interrupted by the starting shot, and we were off. I found myself in the middle of a mob in the open water. Surprisingly, my doubts settled and a sense of inner calm and focus took over.

Just do what you know, Shay. In that moment, the hundreds of hours of laps in the pool and open swim practice came through.

I survived the 1.2-mile swim that day, and was crazy enough (and forgetful enough!) to do it three more times in subsequent races. Every single time as I stand on the sand in the early morning light, waiting...listening...for the starting shot, the same overwhelming doubts rush in and threaten to paralyze me.

I'm certainly not an elegant swimmer, or even a super-coordinated one at that. But if there's one thing I've learned in my triathlon ventures, it's this: **when race day comes, you've got to trust what you know, what is ultimately true.**

To varying degrees, the doubts will be there. Every. Single. Time. The knot in your stomach. The wobbliness in your legs. But the racing thoughts in your head and strange sensations that course through your body aren't the truest measure of reality.

The same is true in our relationship with Jesus. I don't know about you, but when it comes to prayer, I struggle to shake my doubts about God's ability, willingness, presence, and desire for me to come to him.

Is he really listening to little, ordinary me—out of the 7,000,000,000+ people in the world? Maybe he's too busy trying to solve the Middle East crisis or bending his ear to the cry of orphans and widows.

Does he really care? Am I annoying him? Maybe I'm just making a big deal out of nothing and need to pull myself together and figure it out.

Or maybe I've screwed up too badly and he's losing his patience: *You again, Shay? C'mon man. We've been over this like a million times,* I imagine his voice echoing with divine frustration.

Does prayer even make a difference? After all, if God already knows what I need, what's the point?

When these doubts suck me in, I stand paralyzed on the shore of his grace, perhaps dipping my toe in the water with an obligatory prayer, but disconnected from the power of his Spirit. I am the last thing from dangerous. It's not that I don't know what's true—I've read the hallmark passages a hundred times:

- " 'Call to me and I will answer you and tell you great and unsearchable things you do not know' " (JER. 33:3).
- " 'Come to me, all you who are weary and burdened and I will give you rest' " (MT. 11:28).
- "Then you will call on me and come and pray to me, and I will listen to you" (JER. 29:12).

If you've been around church for long, you probably recognize these verses, too. We learned them in Awanas, VBS, and Sunday School, and yet many followers of Jesus struggle to live in these truths. More often than not, we end up praying out of guilt or shame—we know we *should,* but we don't really want to—unless we're in crisis. Then the prayers come fast and heavy. Even people who don't believe in God will cry out to some higher power when their life is on the line. My friends in the military say it really is true that there are no atheists in foxholes.

But what about the rest of the time? I fear that many of us—myself included—can live as though we are functional atheists. Sure, we believe in God. We can point to a dozen Bible passages about prayer. And yet, prayer is far from woven into the fabric of our spiritual lives. It's more like a stray thread here and there. Where's the disconnect? I wonder if, perhaps, it has a lot to do with what we think this divine encounter is all about.

THE HOLY TREKKERS

"How are you?"—"*Good.*" We say these words without even thinking, whether we're actually doing well or having a really rough day. In today's world, prayer is not all that different. It's cultural, like a handshake or a passing greeting. It's something we just *do.* We bless the food (as if eating greasy burgers, but praying beforehand, somehow increases their nutritional value). We may pray before communion or when we hear that a loved one is sick. We shoot up a quick request when we're stuck in traffic or looking for a parking spot.

But is this really prayer? Or a stripped down, cheap imitation of what we were created for? Surely, as Jesus cried out in anguish, his bruised and beaten body struggling for each breath on the cross, he was not envisioning the half-hearted "be with me today" and "bless this food to our bodies" that we call prayer.

Too often, my prayers are quenched by my own doubt before they find their way out of my mouth. They lack potency and conviction, but I kind of sort of pray them anyway. Yet these ho-hum, going-through-the-motions prayers are a far cry from the dangerous prayers we witness in Scripture.

Prayer parted the Red Sea and made the sun stand still. Prayer provided food in the desert for an entire nation. Prayer empowered an ordinary shepherd boy to kill a giant. Prayer transformed a few loaves and fish into a feast for thousands. Prayer enabled a fisherman to walk on water in the middle of a storm. Prayer healed lepers and lame men. Prayer gave sight to the blind and cast out demons. Prayer brought dead people back to life and emboldened followers of Jesus to lay down their lives.

This is not a sweet Sunday School prayer life. Prayer is war, plain and simple. "For though we live in the world," Paul writes, "we do not wage war as the world does." All those doubts we have about God? Paul addresses them head-on (2 COR. 10:3-5):

> *The weapons we fight with are not the weapons of the world. On the contrary, they have divine power to demolish strong holds. We demolish arguments and every pretension that sets itself up against the knowledge of God, and we take captive every thought to make it obedient to Christ.*

What does this look like practically? As a young Christian in ministry, I was intrigued by the story of Leonard Ravenhill, part of a group known as the Holy Trekkers. These men walked the length and breadth of England throughout the 1930s and 40s, holding revivals that led many to Christ. The Holy Trekkers pushed a cart through the war-torn countryside, carrying a giant tent. In the evenings, people would pack into the tent to hear the teaching of God's Word.[1] It sounded pretty cool to me—adventure, ministry, and backpacking Europe? *Count me in!* I only wished I could time travel so I could join the Holy Trekkers, too. It was a romantic thought until I remembered they backpacked throughout World War II!

"My main ambition in life is to be on the devil's most wanted list," Leonard said.[2] What a guy! His goal was not to be liked or popular. Not to have the most followers on Twitter or make the New York Times bestseller list, but to storm the gates of hell.

And then, this: "**No man is greater than his prayer life**."[3] Ravenhill's words shook my self-assured identity as a spiritual leader.

His challenge was exposing and abrasive. I drew back defensively, running circles of justification in my head. *Prayer doesn't mesh well with my personality...it's not my gifting. I'm glad that worked for you, Leonard, but no so much for me. Sure, I'll pray, but it's not the core of my walk with God. It can't be. I'm a doer by nature. I'll storm the gates of hell. I'm ready. Let's do this...*

Try as I might, though, I couldn't honestly dismiss this truth. My perceived greatness, I realized, was nothing but a mirage. In my pride, I had been taking all the credit for my "godly accomplishments," and hoping others would notice, too. I was far from dependent on God.

Is it not through prayer that we turn to God in repentance? Is it not in prayer that we seek God's grace and forgiveness? Is it not in prayer that we run to him in our desperation? Is it not through prayer that we seek strength in our weakness? Is it not in prayer that we invite God to do what only he can do, by his Holy Spirit—bring dead souls to life?

The credit is not ours to take. Yet we reel in the face of such a statement. We try to theologize our way out of it. It leaves us feeling powerless. We frantically justify our own righteousness, as if there is something—anything—we could bring to God. All our attempts to do good for God and invest in his kingdom ultimately fall short.

I needed revival. Perhaps you do, too.

Revival is a term that many of us shy away from. It brings up images of fiery preachers, big tents, and even bigger guilt trips. Revival, though, is really a matter of the heart. It's about transformation—*the return of strength and importance.*

Revival is ultimately about remembering who we are and who God is. This renewing of our minds changes us from the inside out. Brokenness over sin, gratitude for grace, love for Jesus, hunger for his Word, compassion for others, a desire to pray—these aren't things we can drum up on our own. They are the work of the Holy Spirit.

Maybe joining the Holy Trekkers isn't about finding a time machine. We just need to humble our hearts and come, echoing the earnest humility of the disciples: "Lord, teach us to pray" (LK. 11:1).

EXPANDING OUR SOULS

Remember Joe Schuchardt? God used this broken-bodied little boy to reveal my true spiritual condition: twisted by pride and self-sufficiency, crippled in fear and shame, unable to walk in the glorious reality of the gospel. That summer, Joe's prayers brought revival in my heart and among our entire camp staff. God used Joe's passion as a spark to set our hearts on fire.

Pray in a different way, I sensed the Holy Spirit whispering. I didn't know quite what it meant at the time. Looking back now, I see that God has taken me on a journey that has far less to do with *how* I pray and far more to do with *how much* I love to pray.

Anyone who knows me will tell you how much I love to sleep. My half-serious response, when someone asks me, "How are you?" is "If I was any better, I would be sleeping!"

These days, though, I find myself wishing sleep away because I can't wait to spend time with God. Being woken up in the night by one of our kids is becoming less of an annoyance. It's an opportunity to sit with God, to listen to his voice speaking over me as I rock Piper or Tess.

It's weird, but sometimes I feel bummed when I look at my watch and discover it's only two in the morning. I pray myself back to sleep in anticipation of the alarm sounding, so I can slip into my prayer closet and talk with the God of the Universe again.

Now, don't be impressed. This desire is so foreign to me I certainly can't take on iota of credit. (Remember my argument with super-prayer-guy, Leonard?) I am not a praying man by nature, but what I'm discovering is that God is literally changing my nature. No longer does it feel like a spiritual discipline—prayer feels like breathing.

Let me tell you, if God can give this meat-head a craving for prayer, he can stir up the same desire in you! And more than that, he can't wait to!

"If you want to expand your soul, then learn to pray," my hero Leonard Ravenhill encourages us. (Challenge accepted!) He goes on:

> *How do you learn to pray? Well, how do you learn to swim? Do you sit in a chair with your feet up drinking Coke learning*

*to swim? No, you get down and you struggle. That's how you
learn to pray. Prayer is our strength; prayer generates strength;
it generates vision; it generates power; and the devil will drive
you away from the prayer closet more than anything.*[4]

Prayer is not about putting our money in a heavenly vending
machine to get what we want. It's about struggling. Pushing through
our doubts and fears and experiencing them vanish behind us as
we swim forward in supernatural strength.

Prayer is our life source — it enables us to tap into the true reality
of who God is and who we are. Trying to live without prayer is as
ludicrous as ripping the IV out of your arm, jerking the ventilator
tube from your mouth, and telling God, "I got this" as you take
off down the hall of the hospital. You won't get far.

"I am the vine; you are the branches," Jesus tells us. "If you
remain in me and I in you, you will bear much fruit; apart from
me you can do nothing" (JN. 15:5).

Nothing. Nada. Zilch.

Jesus himself exemplified this pursuit. Time and again, Jesus
slipped away to pray. Why did God in the flesh need to pray?
Why did he choose to pray? Perhaps Jesus denied his divine power
in order to model divine dependence for us: "[T]he Son can do
nothing by himself; he can do only what he sees his Father doing,
because whatever the Father does the Son also does…I have come
down from heaven not to do my will but to do the will of him
who sent me" (JN. 5:19, 6:38). Jesus received his marching orders
from God the Father in prayer. If the Son of God needed to seek
the Father in prayer, how much more so do you and I?

Such dependence makes us dangerous. Satan does everything
in his power to shrink God in our minds and inflate ourselves — just
the opposite of what John the Baptist said: "He must increase,
but I must decrease" (JN. 3:30). To the extent Satan can minimize
prayer and fill our minds with doubts about God, he cripples us
spiritually, cunningly whispering the lie that we can do it on our
own strength.

There are many ups and downs in the journey of faith. Sometimes,
pride rears its ugly head and my passion for prayer wanes, but I
long for my soul to expand to experience more of God. The only

way to learn to pray is to pray. And so I pray. Even, and perhaps especially, when I don't feel like it. This is the kind of perseverance and pursuit that sets the enemy on his heels. He knows that, through Jesus, we have divine power to burn his empire to the ground.

Do we know—really know that? Do we walk in that?

Imagine the exponential effect of our accomplishments if they were multiplied through the power of prayer. Jesus says it plainly, through his brother James, "You do not have because you do not ask" (JAS. 4:2). Our power is not in the words we utter. On the contrary, our prayers are only as powerful and transformative as the one we're praying to.

WHY YOUR THOUGHTS ABOUT GOD MATTER

"All true prayer begins in the recognition of the Father," A.B. Simpson reflects. "The name expresses the most personal and tender love, protection, care, and intimacy; and it gives to prayer, at the very outset, the beautiful atmosphere of the home circle and the delightful affectionate and intimate fellowship of friend with friend."[5]

How do you see God? How do you think he sees you? Wrestling with your answers to these questions may do more to unlock your prayer life than anything in this entire chapter.

When Tess crawls up into my lap, I feel like the luckiest man alive. At two, she's the epitome of soft and cuddly and cute. As my little girl babbles on, often, she doesn't make much sense. It doesn't matter, though. Her voice is so precious to me that I gobble it up—I cherish every moment and I can't get enough. And so it is with our prayers. They don't have to sound biblical or theological or smart or fancy.

The beauty of the gospel is that we can come to God exactly as we are. We can crawl up in his lap and tell him what's on our minds and hearts. Stop for a moment, and let it really settle in: the God of the Universe cherishes your words. Every need, every sorrow, every fear. Every aching plea. Even when you're angry, upset, or confused—he longs for you to come to him.

Prayer enables us to tap into the truest reality: that God is a loving Father who longs to connect with us as his children. It brings him great joy. We are not an obligation to him, like a whiny kid he is trying to appease. Far from it! "For the LORD *takes delight* in his people; he crowns the humble with victory" (PS. 149:4, emphasis mine). And again, "The LORD *takes pleasure* in those who fear him, in those who hope in his steadfast love" (PS. 147:11, ESV, emphasis mine).

The natural outcome of dwelling in this truth is movement toward God—boldly approaching God's throne of grace, confident that his mercy, grace, and forgiveness are there for the taking (HEB. 4:16). Bringing our anxieties, worries, and fears to him (1 PET. 5:7). Resting in him as our refuge and strength, even in the midst of suffering, loss, and hardship (PS. 46:1).

Our prayers have dangerous power to demolish, destroy, and wreak havoc to Satan's plans, but too often, this spiritual weapon goes unused because of bad theology. Theology is not just for pastors or folks in seminary. Simply put, theology *is our thoughts about God.* If you think about God, you are practicing theology. And when we practice bad theology, we live out of it, pray out of it, and act out of it.

For most of my life, I approached prayer a lot like blowing bubbles with my kids. The words came out of my mouth, hung in the atmosphere for a moment, and then—poof!—vanished into thin air. I found myself praying things over and over again, like I had to remind God, or else he would forget. Without even realizing it, my incomplete theology was getting in the way of truly connecting with God. I wrongly assumed that the Creator of the Universe is like me. I forget things. Quickly. (Just ask my wife!) But God isn't limited like us. In fact, it's impossible for him to forget!

Rather than wearing ourselves out blowing prayer bubbles, the Holy Spirit invites us to step into a whole new world just beyond our senses—the throne room of heaven. God Almighty sits on his throne, surrounded by twenty-four elders. And you're there, too. Don't believe me?

Here's how the apostle John describes it in his vision: "The twenty-four elders fell down before the Lamb, each holding a harp, and golden bowls full of incense, *which are the prayers of the saints*" (REV. 5:8, emphasis mine).

Your prayers are eternal. They don't disappear into thin air. Nor do they disappear a week, a month, a year, or a lifetime later. On the contrary, they find their way to the epicenter of all power, dominion and authority. They will endure in God's presence long after your time on this earth is through. No wonder prayer is such a dangerous thing in the spiritual realm! Prayer is living and moving, powerful and strong—and Satan can't do anything to shut it down—except convince you not to pray.

John's vivid description continues: "The smoke of the incense, together with the prayers of God's people, went up before God from the angel's hand" (REV. 8:4). In the same way that incense offers a fragrant aroma, your prayers are a delight to God. More than that, they also play a key role in his kingdom coming on this earth.

Do you sometimes doubt that prayer is really *that* powerful? I do. But take a look at this! Describing the scene in the heavenly throne room, John reports, "Then the angel took the censer, filled it with fire from the altar, and hurled it on the earth; and there came peals of thunder, rumblings, flashes of lightning and an earthquake" (REV. 8:5). Wow. God takes the historical sum of the prayers of the saints and drops prayer bombs on the earth in judgment.

Don't let Satan deceive you for one second with that prayer bubble madness! Your prayers matter—not just for today, but also for eternity. God hears and cherishes and is moved by every single one of them. He invites us to "pray without ceasing" (I THESS. 5:17) not because he forgets, but because he longs for us to join in on his kingdom coming and his will being done.

The prayers of the saints lay down a godly infrastructure across space and time throughout the spiritual realm. Prayer does not pass away. Prayer does not deteriorate. Prayer remains because it was established by the everlasting God. In his sovereignty, God has chosen to weave the prayers of mankind into the fabric of his plan.

The weapon of prayer is unleashed through good theology. "So we fix our eyes not on what is seen, but on what is unseen, since what is seen is temporary, but what is unseen is eternal" (2 COR.

4:18). I can't think of any other activity that has the potential to be as rewarding, rich, and eternally meaningful.

DANGEROUS DOESN'T MEAN GLAMOROUS

As we delve more deeply into the spiritual practice of prayer, we must guard against pride and self-righteousness. Jesus had some pretty harsh things to say about the religious leaders of his day who showed off their prayer lives (MT. 6:5). Prayer is never about earning God's favor, one-upping each other, or manipulating God to get what we want. Certainly, it may include requests, petitions, and intercessions, but prayer is first of all an invitation to be with God. In the words of Sadhu Sundar Singh,

> *Prayer is continual abandonment to God. Prayer does not mean asking God for all kinds of things we want; it is rather the desire for God himself, the only Giver of Life. Prayer is not asking, but union with God. Prayer is not a painful effort to gain from God help in the varying needs of our lives. Prayer is the desire to possess God himself, the Source of all life. The true spirit of prayer does not consist in asking for blessings, but in receiving him who is the Giver of all blessings...* [6]

God is the beginning, middle, and end of our pursuit of prayer. He is the ultimate goal. When we pour out our hearts to him, we can trust that he hears, cares, and is at work behind the scenes, even if we can't see it at the time.

"The prayer of a righteous person is powerful and effective," Scripture tells us (JAS. 5:16). The Greek word for "effective" is *energéō*. Sound familiar? It's the same root from which we get the word *energy*, and is likened to "an electrical current energizing a wire, bringing it to a shining light bulb."[7] When we go to God in prayer, we're abandoning any power of our own. Prayer removes human restraint and energizes us with the Holy Spirit. God's power overcomes all things, but in his divine plan, he allows us to choose whether or not we will tap into that power. Our prayers release supernatural energy—a force that puts electricity to shame.

But let me warn you, it may not look all that glamorous. For Paul, it meant being chained to the royal guard in prison. Writing to fellow believers from his jail cell, Paul's words are a bit surprising: "Devote yourselves to prayer, being watchful and thankful. And pray for us, too, that God may open a door for our message, so that we may proclaim the mystery of Christ, for which I am in chains. Pray that I may proclaim it clearly, as I should" (COL. 4:2-4). Paul was in a dangerous situation in prison, but he leaned into the danger and saw battle potential.

If it was me, I'd write something along the lines of, "Guys, pray that God may open a door to this cell! This place stinks, I'm starving, and the guards are torturing me with their continual presence. Pray that God will blow these doors right off their hinges, so we can hit the road again preaching the gospel. I've got speaking engagements that I can't afford to miss."

Paul asked the Colossians to pray for a door to be opened, but not the door of his jail cell. He implored fellow believers to pray that God would open a door for the gospel. And do you know what God did? In his letter to the Philippians, Paul later reports, "[I]t has become clear throughout the entire Praetorian guard that I am in chains for Christ" (PHIL. 1:13).

The Praetorians were the elite warrior force of Rome, numbering somewhere between 6,000 and 9,000 strong. They had become extremely political, powerful, and influential, so much so that when a Caesar rose to power that they didn't like, they would just assassinate him and put their guy in charge. These were the men chained to Paul one after another. With each passing shift, a new Praetorian got some quality time with our man Paul. Though Paul was the one in chains, those suckers were ultimately the captives. As they waited out their shift, these powerful and influential men had no choice but to listen to the gospel.

God answered Paul's prayer in a mighty way, yet the answer didn't look like we might expect. I wonder how many of Paul's friends prayed for his release from prison, and maybe doubted God when that didn't happen. *Aren't you supposed to be a good Father, God?* They might have wondered. *Where are you? Paul is our leader—we need him out here on the streets, preaching your truth! Do you hear us?*

Do you care that he's suffering? Why would you allow this to happen to someone so committed to following you?

I imagine God smiling across the cosmos and whispering, *Just you wait! I am about to unleash through Paul an influence that you can't even dream of.*

How else could Paul have gained a daily audience with some of the most influential men in all of Rome? Paul couldn't have pulled off such a feat in his own strength. He couldn't have thought it up, and thus, he couldn't take any credit. And lest we be tempted to idolize Paul, let's remember: this is the man who formerly uttered murderous threats against followers of Christ. He stood by as Christians were stoned to death and gave hearty approval.

If you doubt God's ability to change your heart—to give you a hunger and thirst for him and a heart for prayer—think again.

One day in heaven, I think we may be surprised by those who lived as dangerous Christians. Humble, ordinary, down-to-earth saints, quietly locked away in secret places, are wreaking a holy havoc in the landscape of eternity. Honestly, I picture an army of elderly women around the globe driving the devil crazy because of the power attached to their prayers—their frail earthly frames juxtaposed with their threatening spiritual strength. They are on the frontlines of God's army precisely because they have nothing to prove. No ego in the way. No platform to build. Just a passionate God to follow and serve.

The race of this life is far more demanding than any triathlon. It's more grueling than the longest race in the world, which is 3,100 miles, by the way. (I won't be signing up for that one!) Dangerous Christians push through doubt and cast off bad theology to keep pursuing, keep asking, and keep praying—even when God seems silent and prayers seem unanswered.

They are relentless and brave, yet surprisingly ordinary. They are faithful in little things. Dangerous Christians don't seek out fame, applause or approval—they seek God as their daily bread.

CHAPTER EIGHT

DAILY BREAD

In matters of grace you need a daily supply. You have no store of strength.
Day by day must you seek help from above…Never go hungry while
the daily bread of grace is on the table of mercy.
—Charles Spurgeon

"TAKE ME, DADDY! TAKE ME!" Lulu jumped up and down with all
the excitement of a six year old. It didn't take much persuading. As
a hunter and an outdoorsman, I'd been waiting for this moment
for years—to bring my kids under my wing and teach them how
to navigate the woods.

I'd originally asked her younger brother Knox, who enthusi-
astically said "yes!" but felt a little uneasy when it was time to go.
By nature, Lulu is pretty quiet and cautious, so her impassioned
plea surprised me a bit.

"Well, honey, there are a few things you should know." I got
down on her level. "Hunting might be pretty cold. We're going
to walk out in the woods, climb up into a tree, and sit there real
still and quiet—for a long time. Maybe a whole hour or two."

Despite my less than glamorous description, Lulu was not to
be deterred. I slipped one of my camo shirts over her head and
wrapped a belt around her waist. She was thrilled about her new
dress, and my camo hat swallowed up her little head.

Lulu and I snuck off into the woods together, both giddy with
expectation. We stopped at the bottom of the chosen tree and
looked up, up, up—twenty feet above us to the stand perched
in its branches.

"Wow, Daddy. That's really high." Lulu's voice quivered a bit.

I was afraid my little girl would bail, but I was wrong. It's not that Lulu wasn't afraid—but she knew she wasn't alone, and that gave her courage. Without a moment's hesitation, she climbed onto my back and wrapped her arms and legs tightly around me. Tying a rope to secure her body to mine, I started climbing.

Never before have I been so keenly aware of every move. *One misstep, and this could end badly.* I moved slowly and steadily from one foothold to the next, Lulu's vice grip a constant reminder of her sweet dependence. Crawling into the stand, we both breathed a sigh of relief as we surveyed the clover field below.

Lulu listened with wide-eyed wonder as I began to teach her the basics.

"When deer come along," I whispered, "if you can see their eyes, they can see you. So you've got to be completely still. All you can do is move your eyeballs. You can't say a word."

As the afternoon sun filtered through the trees, we whispered and giggled and snuggled up to stay warm. We carved our names in the tree. This Daddy's heart was about to explode with joy. These are the moments I live for.

We waited. And waited some more—an hour and a half to be exact, eyes peeled for any sign of movement below us. As the sun dipped behind the Ozarks, my hopes waned. I tied up my bow and began lowering it down. Time to head home for dinner.

Of course, as soon as my bow touched the ground, three deer meandered into the field just ahead. Oblivious of our presence, they were enjoying their clover dinner.

"Lulu, here they come," I whispered ever so faintly, scrambling to get my bow back in my hands. I took aim…and nailed one.

Lulu was ecstatic. "We just shooted a deer!" she erupted in typical Ozarkian grammar, her teeth chattering. The temperatures were quickly dropping, so we opted to track it in the morning light. At daybreak, the whole Robbins family—all seven of us—bundled up and set out to bring home our prize. Lulu lead the way as we followed the trail.

"I found it!" she gleefully exclaimed, dancing around our catch.

I bent down and started cleaning the deer right then and there.

My little girl was by my side, her attention riveted. She followed my directions perfectly, holding each bag as I filled it with venison. Her face beaming with pride, Lulu insisted on helping carry the meat home.

Throughout our hunting excursion, what struck me most was my little girl's undivided focus and unwavering expectation. Lulu hung on to every word that came out of my mouth, and as a result, she got to taste the sweet victory of abiding in her father.

I wonder…what would it look like for us to pursue our Heavenly Father with the same passion and intentionality?

To approach God each day with excitement and expectation, begging him, "Take me, Daddy! Take me on an adventure deeper into your presence!" To cling to him in total dependence, rather than trying to go through life in our own strength.

YOU CAN'T STOCKPILE MANNA

"I have been driven many times upon my knees by the overwhelming conviction that I had nowhere else to go," Abraham Lincoln reflected. "My own wisdom and that of all about me seemed insufficient for that day."[1] True intimacy with God in prayer begins where self-sufficiency ends—the two cannot co-exist. Perhaps this is why the devil works so relentlessly to stroke our pride and ego. He knows that if you and I are connected with God in an intimate, daily relationship, we will become freakishly dangerous weapons of spiritual warfare.

"Blessed are the poor in spirit," Scripture admonishes, "for theirs is the kingdom of heaven" (MT. 5:3). The Greek word for "poor"—*ptóchos*—literally means "to crouch or lower like a beggar."[2] Here's the reality that Satan works overtime to make sure you don't live in: you and I are "deeply destitute, completely lacking resources."[3] When we lean into and fully acknowledge our own spiritual poverty, we open the door to the source of all riches in Jesus.

We have nothing; yet we have everything. This beautiful, disorienting reality drives us to our knees, stripping us of any confidence in our own abilities as we come before Jesus.

"Our Father in heaven, hallowed be your name" (MT. 6:9). In teaching his disciples to pray, Jesus begins here. Not with fancy theological language, but the plea of children who desperately need their daddy. We unlock the power of prayer by reminding our wayward hearts of who God really is. Not a genie in a bottle or a divine Santa Claus, but the Creator and Sustainer of everything. Our God "is before all things, and in him all things hold together" (COL. 1:17). In essence, we're saying, "God, you rule the entire universe. I do not. You are huge and I am small. You are all-powerful and I am all-dependent." This declaration dethrones self-sufficiency and strips Satan of his power.

"Your kingdom come," Jesus continues, "your will be done, on earth as it is in heaven" (MT. 6:10). Right now, this world is the territory of Satan, but God is in the process of restoring all things to their rightful place under his sovereign rule. And it starts with you and me — as we daily choose to live in obedience to our King. This divine conversation isn't about twisting God's arm to get what we want — on the contrary, it's saying, "From my limited perspective, I can't see what is best for me. Whatever your will is, my answer is *yes*. I open up my hands to accept whatever you give. I trust you." Prayer changes us, bringing our hearts into alignment with his will as we loosen our grip on control.

Out of this transformative posture of our hearts flows a simple request, "Give us this day our daily bread" (MT. 6:11). As the Israelites were starving, God provided manna to sustain them in a dry and barren wilderness, but his instructions were clear: " 'I will rain down bread from heaven for you. The people are to go out each day and gather enough for that day' " (EX. 16:4). When Elijah was running for his life, God sent ravens to deliver bread and meat each morning and evening (1 KI. 17). Praying over a few loaves and fish, Jesus multiplied one boy's lunch to feed thousands of hungry people (MT. 14:13-21). In each of these situations, God provided exactly what was needed for the moment — not for next month or next year.

As Jesus shared one last meal with his disciples before his crucifixion, he picked up bread, broke it into pieces, and encouraged them, " 'Take, eat; this is my body' " (MT. 26:26). Daily bread is not ultimately food on the table or money in the bank. It's not getting our way or having all our dreams come true. **Daily bread is nothing less than Jesus himself.** You and I need Jesus just as much — no, even more — than we need a steady intake of calories and protein, fruits and vegetables, vitamins and minerals to be physically fit. The daily bread of a personal, intimate, ongoing conversation with God equips us to be strong and resilient to Satan's attacks.

When the Israelites tried to stockpile manna, they were sorely disappointed to find it moldy and bug-ridden. Trying to stockpile in our spiritual lives doesn't work either. We can't thrive and grow as dangerous Christians if we rely on a church service or Sunday school or small group to nourish our relationship with God. While meeting with other believers is important, prayer is the "bread and butter" of our walk with God. It's our life source — the practical way we abide in Christ and experience his presence on a day-to-day basis. Prayer is not just asking God for things, it is first and foremost being *with* him.

God longs for us to come to him as we are and discover the Bread of Life. "Whoever comes to me will never go hungry," he promises (JN. 6:35). Jesus Christ is our nourishment, his presence the only sustenance that will truly satisfy.

TAPPING INTO SPIRITUAL ABUNDANCE

Growing up, George Müller often stole his father's money to go out drinking and gambling with friends. Ending up in jail didn't seem to make a difference. When his father sent him off to divinity school, George thought up a brilliant plan. Church-going folk were pretty gullible, so why not use the cover of being a pastor to line his own pockets? I imagine Satan was rubbing his hands together with glee — what better way to steal, kill, and destroy? It was almost as if George had read his mind.

In the early 1800s, orphans roamed the streets of England, begging for spare change and leftover food. I'm sure they were no concern of George's (after all, they had nothing he could steal!) but the heart of God was moved with compassion, and he picked an unlikely vessel through which to work—none other than our buddy, George. Not exactly a prime candidate for ministry, we might think. But perhaps that is precisely the point.

God drew George Müller to himself, and in college he surrendered his life to Christ. As George grew in his faith, his heart was burdened to become a missionary, but he was turned down repeatedly from mission boards due to his poor health. One day, George noticed the street children all around him who were struggling to survive, and a light bulb went on. He had no money, no investors, and no board of advisors, but he pulled out a journal and got on his knees. Certainly, his heart was stirred to help these children, but his vision for ministry was not grounded solely in social justice. More than anything, he desired that his life's work testify to the reality that God is still faithful, still hears, and still answers prayer.

In a radical step of faith, George felt that God was calling him to not even ask for financial support to start an orphanage, but instead, make his needs known only to his Heavenly Father. This act of obedience was a complete undoing of the greed and control that had dominated his life for so many years. Through prayer, God began to completely transform this former thief—changing his character from the inside out as George watched God show up and provide again and again.[4]

George was still human, just like us. He admitted often struggling with prayer, particularly in the first decade of his ministry. At times, he just didn't want to pray. His mind would wander. He would feel overwhelmed by the sheer enormity of needs. He would doubt whether God could or would provide. Maybe you can relate. I know I can! Müller goes on to recount a breakthrough he experienced in his prayer life when he began to see God differently:

> *I scarcely ever suffer now in this way. For my heart being nourished by the truth, being brought into experimental [today we would say "experiential"] fellowship with God, I speak to my Father and to my Friend (vile though I am, and unworthy of it) about the things that he has brought before me in his precious Word. It often now astonishes me that I did not sooner see this point.[5]*

George turned a corner in his prayer life when he began to approach God not just as the provider of his needs, but as his Father and his Friend. Over his lifetime, he recorded over 50,000 specific answers to prayer in his journal, 30,000 of which were answered within the hour or the day.[6] That's more than one answered prayer each day, every single day for sixty years! George's obedience in prayer tapped into the riches of spiritual abundance in Christ. Through his ministry, over 10,000 orphans were rescued off the streets. Not only were these children given a roof over their heads and a hot plate of food, they watched God provide all this, moment by moment. Here is one recounting of how God showed up:

"One morning, all the plates and cups and bowls on the table were empty. There was no food in the larder and no money to buy food. The children were waiting for their morning meal. 'Dear Father,' Müller prayed, 'we thank Thee for what Thou art going to give us to eat.'

"There was a knock at the door. The baker stood there, and said, 'Mr. Müller, I couldn't sleep last night. Somehow I felt you didn't have bread for breakfast, and the Lord wanted me to send you some. So I got up at two in the morning and baked some fresh bread...'

"Mr. Müller thanked the baker, and no sooner had he left, when there was a second knock at the door. It was the milkman. He announced that his milk cart had broken down right in front of the orphanage, and he would like to give the children his cans of fresh milk so he could empty his wagon and repair it."[7]

Prayer opens the door to spiritual abundance. That morning—and I imagine many other mornings like it—God got all the glory. I wonder if, at some point, the devil gave up on George Müller and moved on to more vulnerable prey.

His best thief was now one of God's most dangerous prayer warriors!

COMING WITH NO AGENDA

How I long for the boldness and faith with which George Müller prayed. "This is the confidence we have in approaching God," the apostle John writes, "that if we ask anything according to his will, he hears us. And if we know that he hears us—whatever we ask—we know that we have what we asked of him" (1 JN. 5:14-15). In essence, John is saying, "**Pray believing it's as good as done—that God's answer is already on the way. Because if it's God's will, it'll happen.**" Here's where we can get a bit tangled up, though. In my work with teens and college students at Kanakuk, we talk a lot about God's will...and how to find it.

Should I ask her out? What am I supposed to major in? How do I know if he's the "one"? Do I take this job—or not? Should I step into this ministry opportunity? I get peppered with these questions over lunch and around the campfire and as we trek through the woods. Whatever the specific decision, I hear a common thread in these honest, searching hearts:

What is God's will for my life—and how do I know?

I wonder, though, if perhaps we've been asking the wrong question. In today's culture of iPhones and selfies, it's easy to act as if God's will revolves around *us* and the assets and skills we bring to the table (as if we could add anything to God's awesomeness!). But maybe it's actually the other way around. When we pray, "Show me your will for my life," it's easy to come to God with an agenda in the hopes that he will bless it and give us our way. The danger here is that we can easily misinterpret circumstances as divine guidance and seek out the support of friends who will take our side. We can even cherry-pick Scriptures out of context to try and back up our decision. Countless times I've been guilty of this—I've missed what God had for me because I was so focused on what I wanted.

After all, Satan whispers, *wouldn't a loving God want you to be happy?*

The danger of these lies to keep us in bondage stands in stark contrast to the potential danger we can pose to Satan by dwelling in the truth. In Scripture, we don't see people pining over their "life plan"—we witness them seeking to obey and honor God wherever they find themselves. Perhaps, then, God's will is not some mysterious thing we discover, but the daily discipline of aligning our hearts with God's sanctifying work.

Here are a few examples:

- "[G]ive thanks in all circumstances; for this is God's will for you in Christ Jesus" (1 THESS. 5:18).
- "It is God's will that you should be sanctified: that you should avoid sexual immorality" (1 thess. 4:3).
- "For it is God's will that by doing good you should silence the ignorant talk of foolish people" (1 PET. 2:15).

God's will always involves stepping outside of ourselves, loosening our grip on what we want, and coming into his presence with open hands: "God, whatever your will is, that's what I want to be part of." It means holding tightly to God, and loosely to our plans and dreams. Reflecting on the will of God, George Müller writes:

> *I seek at the beginning to get my heart into such a state that it has no will of its own concerning a given matter. Nine-tenths of the trouble with people generally is just here. Nine-tenths of the difficulties are overcome when our hearts are ready to do the Lord's will, whatever it may be. When one is truly in this state, it is usually but a little way to the knowledge of what his will is.*[8]

Imagine if God gave us everything we wanted—I'd be a sloppy mess! If I gave Knox everything he wanted, my three-year-old would have rotting teeth, shaggy hair, and he would stink from wearing his Buzz Lightyear pajamas for a year straight!

There have been more than a few times in my life where, looking back, I found myself saying, "Thank you, God, for *not* giving me what I asked for. What was I thinking?!" When we really know in the core of our being that God's heart is good, we can trust that he is at work, even when our prayers seemingly go unanswered. So next time you find yourself frustrated or confused—wondering, *God, why didn't you answer my prayer?*—don't buy the lie that God is distant or disengaged. Truth is, he's more intimately acquainted with the aching longings of your heart than you can imagine. Your loving Father won't give you everything you want, but he will certainly provide what you need.

It may not always be sirloin steak, but you can count on daily bread.

FIGHTING TO LIVE IN THE TRUTH

"Is prayer your steering wheel or your spare tire?" Corrie ten Boom challenges us.[9] Prayer is not a minor "add on"—it is *the* thing, the main thing—that drives our experience of intimacy with God. Reflecting on this, Oswald Chambers writes,

> *We tend to use prayer as a last resort, but God wants it to be our first line of defense. We pray when there's nothing else we can do, but God wants us to pray before we do anything at all. Most of us would prefer, however, to spend our time doing something that will get immediate results. We don't want to wait for God to resolve matters in his good time because his idea of "good time" is seldom in sync with ours.*[10]

Are you willing to wait—to surrender your expectations of what God *should* do and what he owes you? To wait on God, we have to trust his character. And trust is smack-dab in the middle of the battlefield for our minds and hearts.

Satan will work tirelessly to twist your thoughts about God. He wants you to think that God doesn't care about your needs. *God gave up on you a long time ago,* he'll taunt you.

Here are four time-tested hand grenades to fight back with:

God is omniscient. He knows everything, so don't think for a second that when you cry out to him, he doesn't hear or respond. God understands your thoughts before you think them and feels your emotions before you're aware of them. He knows every word before it comes out of your mouth. And when you don't have any words, his Spirit intercedes on your behalf.

God is omnipresent. He is everywhere, so don't buy the lie that there is any place so dark or hopeless that he is not there. You can't run far enough to escape God, and you can't out sin his grace. Whether you're lying in bed, driving to work, sitting in class, or in the middle of a major crisis, he's there. Engaged. Listening. And ready to act.

God is omnipotent. He is all-powerful—he can do any-thing—so don't fall prey to Satan's caricature of a wimpy Jesus. With a single word, he created light, galaxies, and all the beauty and richness in our world. He is stronger even than death. Nothing is too hard for him.

God is omnicrazyaboutus. He loves you passionately, so don't for a second believe that you're a burden to him. You're not a pain in his neck — you're the desire of his heart. He cares deeply about your needs and troubles and pain and addictions, your burdens and joys and triumphs and victories. And he'll stop at nothing to take care of you.

Remove any one of these four truths, and your prayer life will end up wobbly, like a chair that's missing a leg. If God is not all-present and all-knowing, what motivation do we have to pray? He may be too busy or out of earshot. If God is not all-powerful, he may genuinely care, but be unable to do anything. And if God is not loving and compassionate, why would we want to go to him? He may not be safe or trustworthy.

We all have doubts about God — it's part of being human. Especially when the people closest to us, those who were supposed to love and protect us, do just the opposite, it can be really tough to live in the reality of God's love. *After all,* the devil whispers, *how could God be any different? He's just like them.* When you find yourself under spiritual attack, Psalm 139 is some of the best ammunition out there to demolish the lies of the enemy:

"O LORD, you have searched me and known me!" the psalmist declares (PS. 139:1). God didn't just notice you in passing — he is intimately acquainted with every detail of your life. Every cry of your heart. Every unfulfilled longing. Every fear and anxiety. Every moment of joy. The Hebrew word for "known" here — *yada* — is the same word used throughout the Old Testament to describe sexual intimacy.[11] The God of the Universe longs to connect with you through prayer with an intensity and desire that causes even the closest human relationship to pale in comparison. Think about a time you felt loved and cared for — and multiply that by infinity!

God was there at the moment of your conception and wove you skillfully together in your mother's womb. Every stroke of DNA and every cell of your body were handcrafted by God. He doesn't just know your personality; he crafted your cellular structure.

God's thoughts toward you are more than every grain of sand

on every seashore. He loves you—not because of anything you have or haven't done, but simply because you're his child. Our loving Father knows what we need before we even ask him, and he delights in taking care of his kiddos (MT. 7:9-11):

> Which of you, if your son asks for bread, will give him a stone? Or if he asks for a fish, will give him a snake? If you, then, though you are evil, know how to give good gifts to your children, how much more will your Father in heaven give good gifts to those who ask him!

Think about it. Doesn't it make sense to trust the only One who stands outside of space and time and sees our lives from beginning to end? Talk about perspective!

PREPARE TO BE ASTOUNDED

As I've been writing this book, God has astounded Ashley and I with answers to prayer that we could never have dreamed up. There is no explanation other than God. Every time he shows up, I'm humbled and brought to my knees in worship—*I just spoke to the God of the Universe and he answered me.* I'm reminded time and again of how real, present, and engaged God is and the dangerous power that our prayers hold.

Many of us approach prayer like putting our hunting gear on, but never actually leaving the house. We kind of expect intimacy with God to "just happen." But that's not the picture Jesus paints: "Ask and it will be given to you; seek and you will find; knock and the door will be opened to you. For everyone who asks receives; the one who seeks finds; and to the one who knocks, the door will be opened" (MT. 7:7-11).

So ask…and keep asking. Seek…and keep seeking. Knock… and keep knocking. Prayer takes intentionality. And it will mean sacrifice—loosening our grip on control and independence, so we can cling to our Father.

I want to challenge you, for the next month, to start your day here: "Go into your room, close the door and pray to your Father, who is unseen" (MT. 6:6). Get alone with God. Pour out your heart to him…and listen for his voice.

Perhaps you've never practiced this kind of intentionality before. Take the risk. Go harder, push deeper. This may be the most dangerous decision you've made in a long time! I would be willing to bet that your faith will explode. In fact, I'd bet all that I own on it, because God's promises never fail.

"Your Father, who sees what is done in secret, will reward you" (MT. 6:6).

But don't get it twisted. We're not talking about a prosperity gospel — becoming rich and famous, driving a fast car or going on fancy vacations. God promises eternal rewards — the breaking of strongholds and addictions, joy in place of mourning, healing of our hearts and our bodies, peace in the midst of suffering, hope when all seems lost.

"Prayer may just be the most powerful tool mankind has," Ted Dekker reflects.[12] What are we waiting for? Let's approach God with the same honesty and eagerness as a child traipsing through the woods toward her first tree stand...

"Daddy, I'm a little scared."

"Don't worry, I'll give you courage. I'm going to put you on my back and carry you."

"But, Daddy, I don't know what to do."

"Don't worry, sweetie, I'm right here by your side. Just hold tight to me."

"What are we going to do at the top?"

"Just you wait, kiddo. Prepare to be astounded."

As dangerous Christians, our prayer life doesn't end with personal intimacy with God. This is just the beginning. As we seek to wreak havoc in the spiritual realm, we also have the privilege of standing in the gap for others through intercession.

CHAPTER NINE

STANDING IN THE GAP

It is in the field of prayer that life's critical battles are lost or won...In prayer we bring our spiritual enemies into the presence of God and we fight them there.
—*John Henry Jowett*

"Where is God in all this?" Our friends Lee and Jennifer desperately longed for a child. For years, week in and week out, our small group prayed over them. Huddled in a circle, our faces often wet with tears, we begged God to act on their behalf.

Nothing. No positive pregnancy test. No baby. Just an empty womb and a gaping hole in their hearts. Meanwhile, kiddos began to outnumber adults among our circle of friends. Ashley and I welcomed children into our family one after another.

As we celebrated each new life, we also wept with them.

It was brutal. Gut-wrenching. It didn't make sense. The Robbins' house was about to burst at the seams with the energy and shenanigans of little ones.

And their home? Empty. Jarringly silent. Achingly still.

Why would God give us such a strong desire to be parents, and then seemingly torture us by not making that possible? We wrestled with our friends through questions for which there were no clear answers. After all, we were crying out to the One for whom nothing is impossible (LK. 1:37), who bends down his ear to listen (PS. 116:2), and who promises to answer while we are still speaking (IS. 65:24). Our experience of God wasn't matching up with what we knew to be true from Scripture. Maybe you've been there—you're banging down heaven's door pleading God to act on your behalf or for someone you love, but your voice is growing hoarse and your soul is growing tired. Whether you scroll through Instagram or look around the room, it seems God is busy blessing everyone else with the exact thing he has withheld in your life.

A child. A spouse. A job. A healthy body.

In the midst of angst, anger, and pain, Lee and Jennifer made the courageous choice to be honest. To keep showing up, keep pouring out their hearts with us to God. Because they didn't shrink back in pride or shame, our small group had the privilege of sitting together and seeking God in the midst of dark and painful places—to intercede for and with them.

"Let him who walks in darkness and has no light trust in the name of the LORD and rely on his God" (IS. 50:10, ESV). What does it look like to trust in the darkness? To rely on God when you're not even sure where he is or who he is? I think a big part of it happens in community—praying for and with each other, believing when our friends are losing hope, speaking truth over our brothers and sisters' weary hearts, and sitting with them in the questions.

We didn't know what God was up to, but as a group we pressed into his presence to seek his will. For seven years we prayed, "God, if it's your will, please give Lee and Jennifer a child," but never in a million years could we have guessed how God would answer. As we started praying, unbeknownst to any of us, a little boy was conceived. Due to a series of tragic circumstances, he was placed in foster care. As our friends ached for a child to love and nurture, this little guy ached to belong…for a place to call home.

Those years of waiting re-shaped their desire, though. No longer was having a child about feeling significant or building a perfect little family. At the end of the day, only one thing mattered to Lee and Jennifer:

God, whatever you have for us, our answer is "yes."

That was a dangerous prayer. Yes to accepting the limitations of their own bodies. Yes to the messiness of welcoming a hurting child into their home. Yes to baggage. Yes to complications. Yes to wounds that only God could heal. I believe our friends were only able to say "yes" to welcoming this little boy as their son because God had refined their faith in the furnace. Seven years of waiting loosened their grip on "what I want," and they came before God with open hands and unwavering trust.

No words can describe the excitement we felt to finally meet the fruit of our prayers!

More recently, a new couple in our small group asked for prayer. They, too, were struggling to get pregnant. Despite this, Walter and Jane felt moved to pray for twins, and our community joined with them. After several months of praying and waiting and seeking, Walter and Jane had some big news to share—they were expecting twins.

I can't tell you why God answered our prayers differently—why one family waited seven years, and another just a few months. Why one family welcomed a rambunctious six-year-old into their home, while another couple cradled two tiny newborns.

But I do know this—in both cases, God answered. And not only did he answer, he changed all of us along the way. Interceding together grew our faith. It taught us to come alongside our friends and believe for and with them. To persevere like the four men who tore the roof off a house to get their friend to Jesus (MK. 2:1-12). **Intercession made us one.**

Charles Bent described it best as "loving our neighbor on our knees."[1]

GOING TO BATTLE FOR THOSE WE LOVE

"I'll be praying for you." How easy it is say the words without even thinking, much less stopping our busy lives to come before God's throne on behalf of a family member or friend who is struggling. Not just once, but for the long haul—weeks and months and years on end.

What does it really look like to go to battle for those we love? In the war of prayer, intercession is the front lines. As we grow in our relationship with Jesus, we begin to more instinctively bring our needs to God—to come into his presence confident that he will hear and answer us. That's good. We all need daily bread. But this is just the beginning, the "basic training" that equips us for greater spiritual warfare. God also calls us to bear one another's burdens (GAL. 6:2) and build each other up (1 THESS. 5:11).

Intercession literally means "to intervene on behalf of another."[2] It is pushing back in righteous indignation against the darkness and brokenness of this world and calling on God to act. Through intercession, we groan together in the pains of childbirth as we await the fulfillment of the gospel, clinging to the hope that "the creation itself will be liberated from its bondage to decay and brought into the freedom and glory of the children of God" (ROM. 8:21-22). In the midst of suffering and tragedy, we cling to the unshakeable reality that everything sad will ultimately come untrue, as Samwise Gamgee reflects in J.R.R. TOLKIEN's *The Lord of the Rings*.[3]

"You cannot truly intercede through prayer if you do not believe in the reality of redemption," Oswald Chambers writes. "Instead, you will simply be turning intercession into useless sympathy for others."[4] Good vibes, warm thoughts, and well wishes won't cut it. Intercession is picking up the Sword of the Spirit and warring on behalf of our brothers and sisters. Refusing to let Satan win. Saying, like Sam did to Frodo, "I can't carry it for you, but I can carry you!"[5] Chambers continues,

> *True intercession involves bringing the person, or the circumstance that seems to be crashing in on you, before God, until you are changed by his attitude toward that person or circumstance . . . Our work is to be in such close contact with God that we may have his mind about everything, but we shirk that responsibility by substituting doing for interceding. And yet intercession is the only thing that has no drawbacks, because it keeps our relationship completely open with God. What we must avoid in intercession is praying for someone to be simply "patched up." We must pray that person completely through into contact with the very life of God. Think of the number of people God has brought across our path, only to see us drop them! When we pray on the basis of redemption, God creates something he can create in no other way . . .*[6]

The life of faith is not a journey we take solo. As followers of

Jesus, we are all part of his Body: "If one part suffers, every part suffers with it; if one part is honored, every part rejoices with it" (1 COR. 12:26). God calls us to pray people "completely through," not just to try to patch them up or help them feel better. We have the opportunity to pray our friends and loved ones through to encountering God in the midst of adversity and trials. It's the difference between asking Jesus to calm the storm, like the disciples did, and stepping out like Peter to discover Jesus *right in the middle of it*. Redemption in our friends' and family's lives is often won by blood, sweat, and tears — by crying out to God on their behalf.

Intercession may frustrate you, especially when it seems like nothing is happening. "What the heck! Do my prayers even matter?" God and I have shared more than a few such conversations, yet I have found these moments to be fertile soil for faith to sprout up and trust to blossom. You may often find yourself in dangerous places along the way. Prayer will break your heart as you sit with the evil of this sinful world, but it will also disciple your soul to be moved with compassion, rather than viewing other people's problems as a nuisance. "We never know how God will answer our prayers, but we can expect that he will get us involved in his plan for the answer," Corrie ten Boom reflects. "If we are true intercessors, we must be ready to take part in God's work on behalf of the people for whom we pray."[7]

The transformative potential of intercession makes Satan tremble, but it's not all that popular. Just ask Ezekiel.

NOT ON MY WATCH

Taken hostage from Jerusalem and exiled to Babylon, Ezekiel's calling was to remind the other Israelites of how they got there — by sinning against God. Back in Palestine, where the city walls lay in ruin, Jeremiah shared a similar message, urging people to repent and warning of impending disaster. Speaking through his servant Ezekiel (22:29-31, NASB), God has some scathing words for his people, but also a glimmer of hope:

> *"The people of the land have practiced oppression and committed robbery, and they have wronged the poor and*

needy and have oppressed the sojourner without justice. I searched for a man among them who would build up the wall and stand in the gap before me for the land, so that I would not destroy it; but I found no one. Thus I have poured out my indignation on them; I have consumed them with the fire of my wrath; their way I have brought upon their heads."

"**I found no one.**" These words cut me to the heart every time. "You have not gone up to the breaches in the wall to repair it for the people of Israel so that it will stand firm in the battle on the day of the LORD" (EZEK. 13:5). Broken down walls left Israel vulnerable to attack from the Babylonians. But more than a Jerusalem makeover, God's people needed a spiritual wall of protection. God was looking for men and women of faith to stand amidst the rubble and fight back against the stealing, killing, and destroying work of the devil.

In the story of Ezekiel, I am struck by God's willingness to shower mercy in response to the earnest petition of just one person. "The Lord is not slow about his promise, as some count slowness, but is patient toward you, not wishing for any to perish but for all to come to repentance" (2 PET. 3:9, NASB). God's Word shows us time and again that he may relent from judgment if even one man or woman is willing to stand in the gap and repent on behalf of many.

Abraham begged God not to destroy Sodom (GEN. 18:16-33). Moses interceded on behalf of the Israelites, saving them from a just dose of God's wrath (DUET. 9:18-29). The Levites stood in the gap, making daily sacrifices to atone for the sin of the nation (LEV. 9). Each of these faithful people foreshadowed the ultimate gap filler—Jesus Christ (HEB. 7:24-25, ROM. 8:34):

[B]ecause Jesus lives forever, he has a permanent priesthood. Therefore he is able to save completely those who come to God through him, because he always lives to intercede for them…Who then is the one who condemns? No one. Christ Jesus who died—more than that, who was raised to life—is at the right hand of God and is also interceding for us.

By perfectly fulfilling the law and taking the just punishment for our sin, Jesus stood in the gap of our broken-down lives, looked Satan dead in the eye, and said, "Not on my watch!" As followers of Jesus, you and I get to go and do likewise. Spiritual walls all around us are in disrepair. Will God find us willing and committed to intercede on behalf of his people?

It has been said that "prayer is not a preparation for the battle; it is the battle."[8] As our world reels in the wake of tragedy — mass shootings, terrorism, natural disasters, abuse, poverty, racism, brokenness in all its forms — we have an unparalleled opportunity to stand in the gap. Not so much by posting on Facebook or ranting about it, but by getting on our knees.

NEVER GIVE UP

"More things are wrought by prayer than this world dreams of," Alfred Tennyson writes, but that doesn't mean we can always see God at work from our limited human perspective.[9] On the contrary, "As the heavens are higher than the earth, so are my ways higher than your ways," God tells us, "and my thoughts than your thoughts" (IS. 55:9). The gap between God's thoughts and ours is the seedbed of faith. Without the Holy Spirit, prayer is utter foolishness, and even as believers, things can still be pretty fuzzy sometimes. Our minds grapple to comprehend the spiritual realm, as if we're peeking through a keyhole in the door of time.

Even Daniel, the guy who watched God shut the mouth of ravenous lions, was not immune. As an elderly man in Persia, Daniel received a disturbing message from God about the future of Israel. Reeling in the wake of this news, he didn't call together a press conference, write a blog, or tweet about it —he got on his knees.

For three weeks straight, Daniel fasted and prayed. This guy possessed spiritual endurance and fortitude that I long for. Twenty-one days of crying out to God, with seemingly no response, yet he kept interceding! Talk about a dangerous warrior!

Standing on the banks of the Tigris River, Daniel saw a figure walking toward him. But this was no ordinary messenger. Dressed in white linen, the angel's face was like lightning and his eyes were flaming torches. His entire body glowed like emerald, and his muscular arms and legs shone like polished bronze. He spoke with the authority of an entire army (DAN. 10:11-14):

"O Daniel, man greatly loved, understand the words that I speak to you, and stand upright, for now I have been sent to you . . . Fear not, Daniel, for from the first day that you set your heart to understand and humbled yourself before your God, your words have been heard, and I have come because of your words. The prince of the kingdom of Persia withstood me twenty-one days, but Michael, one of the chief princes, came to help me, for I was left there with the kings of Persia, and came to make you understand what is to happen to your people in the latter days. For the vision is for days yet to come."

God was intimately attuned to Daniel's cries. He responded immediately, but just beyond the curtain of Daniel's senses, a grueling spiritual struggle dragged on for three weeks straight. Demonic forces detained this heavenly messenger, engaging him in vicious combat that ultimately required backup from Michael the Archangel. **Think about it: this angel, with his flaming-torch eyes and bronze arms, was empowered to fight by Daniel's persistent prayers**. I wonder, how might the outcome have been different if Daniel gave up after five days of prayer? Or ten? What if he threw the towel in after two weeks?

"Well, I guess God's busier with more important things," he might have concluded. "I mean, if nothing has happened by now, it's obviously not going to happen."

Ever been there? I know I have! Never assume that your lack of *seeing* God at work means he is on vacation. Satan takes full advantage of our limited perspective—we care about today, this moment, while his destructive agenda against God has mounted up across thousands of years of history. God does not *need* us—he has all the power in the world at his disposal! Yet in the war of good and evil that rages on, he has chosen to delegate tremendous influence to our prayers.

"He seems to do nothing of himself which he can possibly delegate to his creatures,"   C.S. Lewis reflects. "He commands us to do slowly and blunderingly what he could do perfectly and in the twinkling of an eye…Creation seems to be delegation through and through. I suppose this is because he is a giver."[10]

Through intercession, we partner with God to push back evil, to bind Satan's hands with the truth of the gospel and set spiritual captives free. Prayer is not limited by time or space — it doesn't burn out like a candle or wear out like your running shoes. **Prayer is eternal. It gains momentum in the spiritual realm, releasing God's power to wreak havoc — weeks, months, and years before we are often aware of it**. The devil will capitalize on that "in between" time, though, tempting us to give up. To keep fighting, we must remember the ultimate goal of prayer: not to see certain results, but to be with God, to join him in the epic battle for the souls of men and women all around us. We never know what is happening in the spiritual realm, but God does. Intercession is like pouring gasoline on the fire of his kingdom coming. It's dangerous.

So next time you're feeling discouraged and beaten down, remember Daniel. When your arms ache and your heart grows weary, remember how one man's fervent intercession burst open the floodgates of heaven with angelic reinforcements.

Your prayers have the same power.

THIRTY-THREE ANSWERS

I woke up feeling defeated. It was a few weeks into my first summer leading Kanakuk's elementary-aged camp, known as "KI." After nine years working with teenagers, my wife Ashley and I made the transition to head up KI, and to be honest, I was struggling. Big-time. I felt unsure of myself, overwhelmed, and disconnected from God.

Am I even walking intimately with you, God? Did Ashley and I hear you wrong? My mind raced with a slew of questions as I rushed to our morning gathering. The campers were chomping at the bit to start zip-lining, canoeing, and tubing. The only thing standing between this group of rowdy boys and all the "fun stuff" was our morning devotion. Almost flippantly, I opted to give a simple gospel presentation. (With all this pent-up energy, it seemed best to go with something that wouldn't take too long.) To my surprise, the campers quieted themselves down and seemed to hang on to every word.

Dismissing the kids to their next activity, I invited anyone who wanted to talk more about Jesus to join me in our outside church area. Looking back, I noticed a crowd of campers following me.

"No boys, cabins one and two to the football field, cabins three and four to kickball," I barked with annoyance. The kids looked up with puppy dog eyes.

"Wait...do *all* of you want to hear more about the gospel message we talked about?" To my surprise, the entire group nodded their heads in unison. The boys sat down on the stone benches of our outdoor church, perched atop a hundred-foot cliff overlooking Lake Taneycomo.

"Who has committed their life to Christ, but had a tough year?" Two hands. "Who has never made the decision to give their lives to Christ?" Every other hand shot up.

That morning, the entire group surrendered their lives to Jesus.

Meanwhile, the majority of our staff had met to intercede for our campers. "I was praying that the Spirit of God would sweep through this camp, and two minutes later I heard the bell ringing," one of our staff members told me later in wide-eyed wonder.

At Kanakuk, kids ring a huge bell when they choose to follow Christ. Jesus explained in Luke 15 that all of heaven rejoices when one sinner repents, so this age-old tradition of ours symbolizes getting the party started. Our staff poured outside to find a long line of campers ringing the bell. At ten o'clock in the morning, right then and there, we joined in the heavenly celebration at the birth of childlike faith. **Not just one answer to prayer—but thirty-three!**

I was humbled, blown away at God working in spite of my failures. That day, I was vividly reminded that in the midst of difficulty and discouragement, God loves us and is not far from us. He is always moving and each day, he gives us the opportunity to stand in the gap for others. Whether we take that opportunity or not is up to us.

Jesus encourages us to "always pray and not give up" (LK. 18:1). Will we lean into him and ground our hearts in his promises that we know to be true, even when God seems distant? Will we fight through the lies Satan lobs our way to keep asking, keep seeking, and keep knocking? It helps to begin with the end in mind.

JUST A TOOTHLESS DRAGON

June 6, 1944. Allied forces had spent years preparing for the single most strategic move of WORLD WAR II. Finding an inroad to Europe was critical in order to overpower the Nazis, but that was easier said than done! While the Allies had sheer manpower and resources, Nazi forces had better tanks, guns, and planes, along with a well-fortified position.

Weighing multiple strategies, the Allies opted for a fifty-mile stretch of the French coastline. The Allies targeted five beachheads, each heavily fortified. They knew the casualties would be high, but the beaches of Normandy were their best option.

Early on the morning of June 6, Operation Overlord marked the largest seaborne invasion in history. On D-DAY, 24,000 paratroopers dropped behind the front lines and 156,000 soldiers stormed the beaches. At tremendous cost, the Allied troops broke through enemy lines—over 10,000 brave men gave their lives to win freedom for the rest of the world.[11]

In the months that followed, more than a million Allied soldiers poured through this newly gained foothold into Europe. Once the beaches of Normandy were claimed, leadership on both sides knew that the end of the war was just a matter of time, but the Allied forces did not slow with victory in sight. Every skirmish and battle the Allies chased down resulted in lives being saved and prisoners from concentration camps being rescued.

On April 25, 1945, enemy troops were expelled from Finland.

On April 29, German forces in Italy surrendered; the next day Hitler committed suicide.

On May 2, the Allies took back Berlin.

On May 4, Nazis in northwest Germany, the Netherlands, and Denmark surrendered.

On May 6, Hitler's second officer in command—and the most powerful Nazi official still alive at the time—surrendered to the U.S. Air Force.

Finally, at 2:41 a.m. on May 7, the German Chief of Staff signed documents of unconditional surrender to the Allies.[12]

Ultimately, WORLD WAR II was won on June 6, 1944—when the beaches of Normandy were claimed—yet it was not until nearly a year later that the Nazis formally surrendered. Winning the war was both an event and a process.

The D-DAY of human history took place 2,000 years ago. Jesus Christ stormed the beachhead of Calvary to take back humanity from the grip of Satan. You and I were on his mind—wasting away in concentration camps, tortured by sin, unable to save ourselves. Like so many soldiers on the Normandy coast, Jesus died that day, but he didn't stay dead. Through his resurrection, he defeated death and the grave. The price was paid for our sin and we were rescued from the clutches of spiritual death. Now we get to stand in the gap for others.

The war is won. It's only a matter of time until Jesus returns to restore everything to himself. And Satan knows it: "He is filled with fury, because he knows that his time is short…" (REV. 12:12). Scripture uses the picture of a dragon, bent on destroying the Bride of Christ. "Then the dragon was enraged at the woman and went off to wage war against the rest of her offspring—those who keep God's commands and hold fast their testimony about Jesus" (REV. 12:17). Our enemy scrambles to take as many people down with him as possible. As followers of Jesus, we have been commissioned to aggressively engage in battles and skirmishes. To seek and save the lost during these last days of a war that has ultimately been won.

Every day is precious. Every battle matters. Every fight counts, even when you can't see the outcome. Sometimes power is best found in patience and persistence.

"When Satan was cast down from the heavens, he declared war on the church; that includes you," John Eldredge writes. "We are at war, whether you choose to believe it or not."[13]

But don't lose heart. If we stand in the authority of Jesus, all Satan can do is try to gum us to death. Our toothless foe has no choice but to cower and run. Every time you stand in the gap for someone else, you love that person dangerously. You unleash the power of God. And you bring the gospel to life.

PUSHING BACK DARKNESS

"[P]ray in the Spirit on all occasions with all kinds of prayers and requests," Paul challenges us. "With this in mind, be alert and always keep on praying for all the Lord's people" (EPH. 6:18). One of the things I love most about intercession is that I can wake up and pick a fight with the most powerful super villain of all time and have the upper hand.

You can push back darkness and take territory for Christ today in any battle you care to take the time for. When you look at this broken world, what gets you angry? What battle seems so far out of your league, and yet you long to make a difference? For what cause will you endanger yourself?

Terrorism. Sex trafficking. Pornography. Broken marriages. Orphans. Refugees. Racism. Abortion—you name it. Theses battles feel so overwhelming, and yet, as followers of Jesus, we have the upper hand. We can either stick our head in the sand and try to build comfortable little lives, saying, "It's not that bad," or we can look the brokenness of our world in the face and actively engage it by falling to our knees in intercession.

It's mind-blowing, really. We can wage war halfway across the world without getting on a plane or picking up our phone. We can battle on behalf of the persecuted church in China and our Syrian brothers and sisters who are suffering for their faith. We can enter into the Oval Office and the headquarters of ISIS. We can exert divine influence in the brothels of Bangladesh, the war-torn countryside of Sudan, and the streets of our own cities. We can beg God for justice for the unborn and cry out for mercy on behalf of all those who are oppressed or marginalized.

But it's not just battles on the other side of the world or the country; it's in our own back yard, too. Our communities, workplaces, and classrooms. Our neighborhoods, homes...even our living rooms. Satan prowls around looking for weakness, for broken down walls. Where is there weakness—or potential weakness—in your life? In the lives of those you love?

Find it…and commit to standing in the gap to fight.

Our friends Chuck and Peg were married for sixty years before Chuck went to be with Jesus. I asked eighty-four-year-old Peg for marriage advice and her response was simple, yet profound: "The couple that prays together stays together." Just six weeks after Chuck died, Peg joined him in heaven, but her words stuck with me, fueling my passion for intercession.

Ashley and I pray over our children's teachers and their future college professors. We pray that God's Word will be our kids' ultimate source of truth. We pray for friends who will build them up, and for opportunities to love and serve classmates who don't know God. We pray over the locker rooms that Knox will find himself in—for strength, purity, and a way of escape from temptation. We pray for the men our little girls will one day date and marry. We pray for God to guard our daughters' hearts and show them how precious they are to him. We pray that our children will not be afraid to walk away from a relationship that isn't of God. We pray for our marriage, too. We pray against anything that could drive us apart and destroy our family.

Seriously, any fight you want to pick, you can—through your prayers.

Only in heaven will we fully grasp the power and potential at our fingertips to bring God's kingdom to life in this world. God unleashes his power through the cries of dangerous Christians—men and women who dare to defy Satan, step out in faith, and call on God to do what only he can.

Not out of fear of what will happen if we don't, but passionate belief in what can happen if we do.

DANGEROUS

PASSION

CHAPTER TEN

DISARMING FEAR

Outside of the will of God there is nothing I want. And in the will of God, there is nothing I fear.
—*A. W. Tozer*

ASHLEY'S SCREAMS ECHOED THROUGH THE HOUSE. Whatever the threat, I knew it was serious because it took the air out of her lungs. I peeled around the corner and saw my wife frozen in the doorway.

Just outside, at her feet, a copperhead snake lay coiled up and ready to strike.

Instinctively, I searched for the closest weapon, which happened to be a level leaning next to our front door. In that moment, I was keenly aware of my limited toolbox. I could barely put together a birdhouse with my current tool kit, much less get rid of a poisonous snake.

Jumping in front of Ashley like a human shield, I attempted to pin him to the ground with my level. Angry and threatened, the copperhead reared back to strike me.

"Close the door! Go inside and close the door!" I yelled to Ashley, jumping over the beast and trying to think on my feet. Ashley peeled herself off the front wall and slammed the door just in time.

Time was short. *If I let this snake get away, he remains a threat to my entire family.* With my adrenaline pumping, I spun around to the garage in search of better weapons: a hammer, a garden rake, and a shovel.

To this day, I'm not sure how I carried all of them. Or how I got from the garage back to the front stoop in .5 seconds. The copperhead was slithering along the side of the house by now, searching for someplace to hide. (Sorry to any of you who are copperhead lovers—he was threatening my family!)

With the copperhead locked in my sights, I chucked my hammer, missing him by three feet. Tossing aside the garden rake, I raised the shovel above my head and brought it down with a fury, pinning the snake up against our foundation.

Buzzz. It's wasn't the snake hissing this time. A swarm of carpenter bees poured out of the ground, ready for war. In the midst of the melee, I had managed to drive my shovel right through their nest!

One way or another, it seemed poisonous venom was in my future. But then, an amazing thing happened. Rather than coming after me, scores of bees started attacking the copperhead instead. It felt like the Discovery Channel was happening in my yard. I pulled out my phone to capture it on camera, my fear turned to fascination.

The copperhead that minutes ago struck fear in Ashley's heart and sent me scrambling for suitable weapons now writhed about helplessly. Once the bees had done their part, I moved in and finished the snake off with the rake and shovel. The bees and I saved the day…at least that day. But wherever there's one snake, there could be more.

What if it had been Lulu or Knox at the door, rather than Ashley? What if the snake had been hidden in the grass, rather than in plain sight on the sidewalk?

These days, Ashley and I are extra cautious. Always looking before we step. Keeping the grass short and our eyes peeled when we let the kids loose to play in the yard.

Fear is paralyzing like that. It has the potential to cripple your faith and shut down your passion for God, turning you from a menacing enemy into a quivering fool in the spiritual realm. Fear can stop even the most dangerous Christians in their tracks.

But it doesn't have to.

DON'T BE FOOLED

"For we are not unaware of [Satan's] schemes" (2 COR. 2:11). The biblical imperative is clear: *don't be fooled.* Which means that it's easy to fall prey and perhaps not even know it. To blame it on bad sleep or bad pizza, a bad boss or bad traffic. "How little can be done under the spirit of fear," Florence Nightingale writes.[1] Our spiritual enemy is well aware.

"Most religious people are pretty harmless to us," the devil coaches his evil forces, "but watch out for those people who humble themselves, fall to their knees, and pursue the presence of God. Let the Holy Spirit stir up passion, and you are dead meat. This is what makes them truly dangerous. You will be powerless to stop God's kingdom from advancing.

"This is your mission: Pull out all the stops. Distract them. Lure them away with temptation. Make them busy about things that don't really matter. Puff them up with spiritual pride. Make them indifferent. But most of all, make them afraid. Fear is our greatest weapon."

And he's right. Watch the news or scroll through your newsfeed, and you can't escape the violence and hatred and evil that is a reality in our broken world. It's easy to lose heart. In fact, fear is a natural human reaction to threat. These days, it seems we don't have to look far to find danger and uncertainty. Satan is wreaking havoc on families and marriages and communities and human life itself. If you seek God, the devil will be seeking you.

Edwin Hubbell Chapin reflects, "A man can no more be a Christian without facing evil and conquering it than he can be a soldier without going to battle, facing the cannon's mouth, and encountering the enemy in the field."[2] This is real stuff. The stakes are high. Satan's venom is far more deadly than any copperhead. And he doesn't play fair.

When Jesus commands us in Scripture, "Do not fear," he's not saying, "Chill, guys. Stop freaking out. It's all in your head." Far from it! **It's not that our world isn't scary — it's that our God is more powerful than any challenge or evil we will ever face.**

As dangerous Christians, it's not that we are never afraid. It's that we develop the capacity to recognize fear, fight back, and ultimately disarm it through the Holy Spirit. We learn to put fear in its place at the feet of Jesus, rather than being taken captive by it.

Our spiritual enemy has some mighty strong lungs on him, I tell our campers at Kanakuk. If you imagine fear as a balloon, you'd better believe the devil is blowing it up as big as he possibly can. What started as a hollow rubber pouch that fits in the palm of your hand can quickly start to take up some space in the room. The reality, though, is that balloons are just rubber stretched tight — paper-thin membranes that trap in air. A balloon can be punctured with a pair of scissors, a key... even your fingernail. If all else fails, you can sit on it.

"For God has not given us a spirit of fear, but of power and of love and of a sound mind" (2 TIM. 1:7). The Greek root for "power" is *dunamai.* Sound familiar? It's where we get the word dynamite.[3] In Jesus, you and I have access to spiritual explosives that can blow up the devil's lies and schemes. But that's not all. *Agápē,* the word used here for "love," refers to the unconditional, never-ending benevolence of God toward us.[4] Knowing who you are — a deeply loved and precious child of God — is a critical weapon in this war we're waging. Finally, "a sound mind," or *sóphronismos,* refers to prudent or sensible behavior that stems from godly reasoning.[5]

Each of these three words holds a key to disarming fear, but it might not look like you'd expect. God has a reputation for choosing unlikely heroes. He doesn't need ripped biceps, polished armor, or toned egos to craft a dangerous Christian. God looks at the heart.

BLEEDING OUT HOPE

The Israelites stood confident, jaws set and ready for victory, until a giant stepped out from the enemy ranks. Towering nearly ten feet tall, he wore a bronze helmet and carried a thirty-pound spear. The iron head of his spear alone weighed sixteen pounds. Imagine that sucker whizzing at your head!

And that wasn't Goliath's only weapon. If perchance you ducked to evade his missile-spear, this guy had a javelin slung across his back and a massive sword in his hand. Should you even try to take a shot at him, he was covered in 125 pounds of bronze armor that protected his body from head to toe. Not to mention the gargantuan shield his servant carried in front of him.

Spear. Javelin. Sword. Armor. Shield. This bully was impenetrable, ready to destroy and wreak havoc. And he knew it. "Why do you come out to draw up in battle array?" he mocked the Israelites. "Am I not the Philistine and you servants of Saul? Choose a man for yourselves and let him come down to me. If he is able to fight with me and kill me, then we will become your servants; but if I prevail against him and kill him, then you shall become our servants and serve us" (1 SAM. 17:8-9). The Jewish ranks had no answer for this super soldier. His proposal seemed an obvious trap to re-enslave the Israelites and take away their Promised Land.

With every sunrise, Goliath's cocky voice boomed across the valley, reminding the troops of their impending doom: "I defy the ranks of Israel this day; give me a man that we may fight together" (1 SAM. 17:10). No wonder God's people were frozen in fear. Even King Saul, whom they'd begged God for, wasn't able to rescue them from this invading giant. Their best-laid plans came to nothing, and here they stood on the brink of certain death.

Can you imagine being Saul and watching Goliath saunter out across the valley toward your encampment? At that point, you're probably yelling for Achilles, and your commander responds dejectedly, "Sir, we have no Achilles." Then you yell for Maximus and discover you have no Maximus. You yell for Leonidas, and there is no Leonidas. All you have are Hezekiah and Jedediah and they are both like five feet three inches tall. You've got problems.

"Saul and all the Israelites were dismayed and greatly afraid," Scripture tells us (1 SAM. 17:11). The Hebrew words used here capture the feeling of being beaten down, terrified, utterly shattered, and done for.[6] Imagine waking up every morning with a sinking gut sense of dread. Maybe you do feel that way sometimes—*I don't know how this is going to play out, but it can't end well.*

Morning and evening, for forty tormentful days, this fear-monger paralyzed the Israelites with his words. Goliath knew that his greatest weapon was not that thirty-pound spear, but his ceaseless taunts and insults. No need to cut the army down with his sword; fear sliced through their hearts and left them bleeding out hope.

As your feet hit the floor each morning, what taunts boom across the valley of your mind? Have they left you wounded — hemorrhaging spiritual passion — and powerless to engage in the spiritual battle right in front of you?

SPIRITUAL SEPTICEMIA

After a football injury in high school, my doctor suggested that I take it easy lifting weights. Heeding his advice, I took it down a notch. I was in the middle of deadlifts the next morning when I heard my coach's gruff voice behind me.

"What're you doing, Shay?"

Trying to keep my calm, I explained the back pain I'd been having, and how the doctor had told me to lay off the heavy weights.

Looking me square in the eyes, he sneered, "Are you going to be playing for your chiropractor this year?"

This conversation threw my entire football season into a spiral. His words hurt because I had already given so much, and yet, my best wasn't good enough. Every time I was on the field after that, I could not for the life of me remember the plays I was supposed to be quarterbacking. Nearly twenty years later, his words still come back to haunt me at times like a broken record.

Satan may bully us openly or whisper despair in the corners of our minds. The most dangerous part of all is that too often, we don't even recognize these fear bombs as a spiritual attack. *We just call it "life."*

Who — or what — is your Goliath? We've all had people in our lives speak lies and accusations, sometimes with the same persistence and audacity of this Philistine giant. The enemy dredges up and replays these painful memories and conversations over and over and over again. No longer do we need to hear the actual words from someone else — we tell them to ourselves.

Your best isn't good enough.
You are a failure — just look at all the mistakes you've made.
God could care less about you.

There's no hope.
You're dumb and worthless—no one would want you.

Fear festers in the wounds of life ...like bacteria in a wound that saps our strength and passion. Left untreated, these lies can spread and grow into septicemia—blood poisoning that threatens our spiritual livelihood. For forty days, the battle against Goliath was lost before it even started because, ultimately, it was a battle for the minds and hearts of God's people.

How easy it is for us, like the Israelites, to lose perspective. It has been said, "If you tell a lie big enough and keep repeating it, people will eventually come to believe it."[7]

Words have incredible power to tear down or build up. You and I will inevitably be dominated and controlled by what we think about, meditate on, and take in as truth. Satan is a master at this, and he capitalizes on the brokenness of our world and the imperfect people in our lives to plant seeds of self-doubt and fear.

WHY YOUR HISTORY MATTERS

After so many days of ridicule by Goliath, the Jewish army had been reduced to dead men walking. No one—not even the strongest warrior among them—was any match for this giant, they reasoned. It was only a matter of time until that thirty-pound javelin would pierce every one of them through. But maybe that's where Saul and his army went wrong.

Just a few generations back, these men's ancestors had walked through the Red Sea on dry land and watched God destroy the entire Egyptian army. They had been sustained by Yahweh in the wilderness for not just forty days, but forty years. They had experienced God topple the walls of an entire city and deliver Canaan into their hands when they felt as small and powerless as grasshoppers.

God commanded his people to gather stones of remembrance so they would not forget: "So all the nations of the earth might know that the Lord's hand is powerful, and so you might fear the Lord your God forever" (JOSH. 4:24). Piling up stones of remembrance became a common practice to commemorate Yahweh's rescue and provision. These tangible memorials were intended to combat fear and remind God's people of an earth-shaking truth: **impossible situations—when all seems lost—are precisely the moments when God loves to show up and do what only he can do**.

I wonder, that day in the Valley of Elah, were there stones of remembrance piled up nearby? Did the Israelite soldiers even see them? Fear did its mind-numbing work, and God's people stopped hearing, stopped seeing, and stopped remembering. It seems any memory of God's faithfulness faded into the background amidst the chaos and panic that bred hopelessness.

But when Goliath came out on day forty-one to start up his rigmarole, "David heard it" (1 SAM. 17:23). Sent by his father from Bethlehem to check up on his older brothers, David's mission was simple: deliver ten loaves of bread and ten blocks of cheese, and bring a report back home. A quick trip, while someone else covered his shift with the sheep.

As Goliath's taunts echoed across the valley, the shepherd boy's ears perked up. "What will be done for the man who kills this Philistine and removes this disgrace from Israel?" David asked the soldiers around him. "Who is this uncircumcised Philistine that he should defy the armies of the living God?" (1 SAM. 17:26) I love this kid. No need to be politically correct—he said it like he saw it. David was offended and angry that anyone could get away with talking smack against the God of the Universe.

David had a personal history with God. While his brothers were out fending off national security threats, the baby of the family had been left at home with the grunt work—taking care of the animals. And yet, these non-glamorous, oh-so-ordinary experiences are precisely what shaped David's character, fueled his passion for God, and gave him spiritual confidence. David hadn't just *heard* about this God of Abraham, Isaac, and Jacob—he had experienced God save his life when all seemed lost. Multiple times. And he couldn't forget. The work of Yahweh wasn't a distant memory rooted in stories from generations ago—it was a present reality. David knew that if he feared God, he had nothing else to fear, and that's what made him dangerous.

Stop for a moment, and consider your own history with God. Where are the monuments in your life to the goodness and faithfulness of God that perhaps you've dismissed as just heaps of rocks? And how can you discipline your heart to remember?

"Remember the wondrous works that [God] has done…" the Holy Spirit whispers (PS. 105:5). Don't let Satan win. Put your fears in proper perspective against the power of the Cross. Come into the presence of Jesus — the one who overcame death itself — and you may be surprised to notice that your Goliath begins to shrink.

AN ANTHEM OF COURAGE

"If I could hear Christ praying for me in the next room, I would not fear a million enemies," Robert Murray M'Cheyne writes. "Yet distance makes no difference. He is praying for me."[8] The reality of this truth can make us unstoppable. But Jesus never guaranteed that we'd have a following or a fan club. On the contrary, if you seek to live dangerously as a follower of Jesus, there's one thing you can count on — pushback.

Like sunlight rushing in to a dark room, David's passion breathed hope into the weary Israelite army. And it also made some people pretty mad. Namely, David's older brother, Eliab: "Why have you come down?" he attacked David. "And with whom have you left those few sheep in the wilderness?" (Notice the condescending tone.) "I know your insolence and the wickedness of your heart; for you have come down in order to see the battle" (1 SAM. 17:27-28).

In essence, Eliab was saying, "This is way above your pay grade, pipsqueak. Go home to your sheep and leave the *real* fighting to the men." The devil will enlist anyone he can — even those closest to us — to shut down our spiritual passion and squelch our hope. Thankfully, David didn't take the bait. He knew the real battle wasn't out there facing Goliath — it was right here in the army camp.

"He turned away from [Eliab] to another and said the same thing," the Bible tells us (1 SAM. 17:29). David didn't need to defend himself against false accusations, nor did he get discouraged and give up. His identity wasn't rooted in the approval of others, and it ultimately earned him an audience with the king.

Saul had his doubts, though. "You are not able to go against this Philistine to fight with him; for you are but a youth while he has been a warrior from his youth" (1 SAM. 17:33). The king of Israel, like everyone else, had fallen prey to spiritual amnesia, seeing things from a purely human perspective. The best lies are always mostly true. After all, Saul was just stating the facts right? Goliath had a long history of battle-wins. He'd been an infamous military hero far longer than David had even been alive!

Fear bombs were coming at David from every direction. *You're a wimp. This is way out of your league. Give up and go home.*

"Do you know who Goliath is?" Perhaps Saul hoped to speak some sense into this zealous teenager. "It's a suicide mission, trying to fight him."

"I get it, but do you remember who our God is?" This kid had no ego to prove, no personal need to be a hero. He just took God at his word. David's secret sauce was simple: **his posture of humility fueled his pursuit of God, that intimate day-to-day relationship produced spiritual passion, and that passion made him dangerous**. David wasn't just zealous; he had evidence to back it up (1 SAM. 17:34-37):

> *"Your servant has been keeping his father's sheep. When a lion or a bear came and carried off a sheep from the flock, I went after it, struck it and rescued the sheep from its mouth. When it turned on me, I seized it by its hair, struck it and killed it. Your servant has killed both the lion and the bear; this uncircumcised Philistine will be like one of them, because he has defied the armies of the living God. The Lord who rescued me from the paw of the lion and the paw of the bear will rescue me from the hand of this Philistine."*

With one audacious statement, this teenage kid popped the ever-growing balloon of pandemonium. "I learned that courage was not the absence of fear, but the triumph over it," Nelson Mandela reflects. "The brave man is not he who does not feel afraid, but he who conquers that fear."9

I wonder, that day, what empowered David to conquer his fear? Did he look over and see a pile of stones stacked up in memory of God's faithfulness? Did he reach up and fiddle with the bear claw hanging from a leather strap around his neck? Did he look down and notice the scars on his forearms, a sobering reminder of his fight with the lion?

Regardless, his testimony was clear: "Whether I'm in the pastures of Bethlehem wrestling a wild animal or in the Valley of Elah facing a giant makes very little difference—because God is here. Right now. My God is powerful and he is unchangeable. He bends his ear to rescue and protect his children."

That was David's anthem of courage. What about yours?

FAITH THAT DEFIES ALL REASON

"The presence of hope in the invincible sovereignty of God drives out fear," John Piper writes.[10] How can you and I wage war against our giants of fear? Saul had a brilliant idea—he offered David his own bronze helmet and suit of armor—arguably the best in the nation. But the weight of the chainmail and the king's expectations was cumbersome and unwieldy. It might look cool and intimidating, but it would only slow him down.

This warrior's soul was protected by armor far more impenetrable than iron and bronze. The promises of God were his first defense, not his last resort. David's greatest weapon was faith—"the assurance of things hoped for, the conviction of things not seen" (HEB. 11:1). Even when it didn't make sense, even when he wasn't sure exactly *how* God would rescue, one thing was certain—God *would* show up. Because David made God his stronghold, the devil did not have even a pinky toe's worth of footing in his life.

"Am I a dog, that you come at me with sticks?" Goliath mocked. "Come here," he said, "and I'll give your flesh to the birds and the wild animals!" (1 SAM. 17:43-44). Confronted by the force field of faith, Satan's best fear bombs evaporated into thin air.

Sure, Goliath was still intimidating. But David put fear in its proper place against the backdrop of an all-powerful God (1 SAM. 17:45-46):

> David said to the Philistine, "You come against me with sword and spear and javelin, but I come against you in the name of the Lord Almighty, the God of the armies of Israel,

*whom you have defied. This day the Lord will deliver you
into my hands, and I'll strike you down and cut off your head.
This very day I will give the carcasses of the Philistine army
to the birds and the wild animals, and the whole world will
know that there is a God in Israel. All those gathered here
will know that it is not by sword or spear that the Lord saves;
for the battle is the Lord's, and he will give all of you into
our hands."*

Oh to have this kind of boldness and God-confidence in con-
fronting our own giants. Seeing Goliath in light of God's faithfulness across thousands of years—and in his own life—bolstered
David's faith to do the impossible. Rather than running away or
shaking in his boots, David charged straight toward Goliath. I
imagine the Israelite army looked on in horror as this kid was
about to get murdered.

Thwack! Wait, what just happened? Everybody was confused,
except David. With a sling, a single stone, and faith that can
topple giants, this shepherd boy knocked Goliath smack-dab in
the forehead. Hundreds of pounds of armor came crashing down
in a heap.

I wonder if perhaps this scene was on David's mind when he
later penned these words: "The Lord is my light and my salvation—whom shall I fear? The Lord is the stronghold of my life—of
whom shall I be afraid? When the wicked advance against me to
devour me, it is my enemies and my foes who will stumble and
fall" (PS. 27:1-2).

That day, David defeated Goliath without a sword in his
hand—he used Goliath's own sword to finish the job off. You
see, when we truly live in the reality that the battle is the Lord's,
we realize that our enemy is utterly powerless against the promises
of God. In fact, we can use his own tactics against him.

All those lies Satan whispers in your mind? All those failures,
sins, and mistakes he won't let you forget? Let the devil's taunts
drive you to even more radical trust in Jesus, to deeper intimacy
with your Heavenly Father, whose "perfect love drives out fear"
(1 JN. 4:18).

A DANGEROUS PRAYER

"I pray that out of his glorious riches he may strengthen you," Paul writes, "with *power* through his Spirit in your inner being" (EPH. 3:16, emphasis mine). *Dunamai.* Remember that word? The same Greek root is used here for "power." Our Heavenly Father doesn't just promise a pat on the back, he offers endless storehouses of spiritual dynamite. Through the Holy Spirit, this divine power is there for the taking. But it's not a download or a delivery. It's a person.

"[S]o that Christ may dwell in your hearts through faith," Paul continues. "And I pray that you, being rooted and established in *love,* may have power, together with all the Lord's holy people, to grasp how wide and long and high and deep is the *love* of Christ" (EPH. 3:17-18, emphasis mine). *Agápē.* Not a love that we earn like a purple heart for our courage in battle, but the passionate desire of your Heavenly Father for you, his child, even in the moments when fear gets the best of you.

But that's not all. Paul prays that you and I would "know this love that *surpasses knowledge*—that you may be filled to the measure of all the fullness of God" (EPH. 3:19, emphasis mine). In his previous admonition to Timothy, Paul referenced a *sound mind* as an antidote to fear (2 TIM. 1:7). Here, he takes it one step further. This power, this love, is actually beyond comprehension. It's not a skill we can develop by sheer reason or willpower. It's a gift.

Our passion, our power, our love… is all just a spillover of God's riches. Perhaps this is what fueled Paul's radical declaration: "For Christ's sake, I delight in weaknesses, in insults, in hardships, in persecutions, in difficulties. For when I am weak, then I am strong" (2 COR. 12:10).

The battle is the Lord's. This truth echoes across thousands of years—from the Valley of Elah to Paul's prison cell in Rome—to this very moment. John Eldredge reminds us,

> *The Enemy fears you. You are dangerous big-time. If you ever really got your heart back, and lived from it with courage, you would be a huge problem to him. You would do a lot of*

*damage...on the side of good. Remember how valiant and
effective God has been in the history of the world? You are
a stem of that victorious stalk.*[11]

Perhaps the most dangerous prayer of all is the one that Jesus
Christ is praying over you right now: "My prayer is not that you
take them out of the world but that you protect them from the
evil one" (JN. 17:15). You are protected. You are safe. And every
single wound in your life has the potential to become a weapon.

Fear can paralyze our hearts, or it can become a doorway into
even greater intimacy with God and more destructive combat
against our spiritual enemy.

The choice is yours.

CHAPTER ELEVEN

WOUNDS INTO WEAPONS

We want to avoid suffering, death, sin, ashes. But we live in a world crushed and broken and torn, a world God himself visited to redeem. We receive his poured-out life, and being allowed the high privilege of suffering with him, may then pour ourselves out for others.
—*Elisabeth Elliot*

GROWING UP, I VISITED THE ER MORE TIMES THAN I CAN COUNT, but there's one experience in particular that I'll never forget. The summer before eighth grade, my buddies and I discovered that the horseweeds growing down by our creek had weapon potential.

All we had to do was yank the six or seven foot stalks out of the ground—bulbs and all—and use our pocketknives to sharpen the ends into spears. Then the battle began!

When Matt the bully showed up one afternoon, I was ready to take him on. Matt was a high schooler in our neighborhood who had a reputation of putting pipsqueaks like us in our place. We stared each other down, squaring off like a couple of cowboys in the O.K. Corral. In that moment, my instincts took over…and I chucked my spear at him with all the force a thirteen-year-old could muster!

Alas, my carefully hewn spear bounced off Matt's steel chest. I stood frozen as I witnessed an atomic bomb of fury go off in his eyes. Matt bent over, picked up my spear, and began to chase me down with it! With no way to defend myself, I tucked tail and ran, but he caught up with me in three strides.

Searing pain shot through my leg. I looked down to see my own spear stuck into the back of my calf. It fell out, leaving a bloody, gaping hole the size of a silver dollar.

With a smirk, Matt sauntered off as I tried to stop the bleeding. I took off my shoes, tied a sock around my leg, and hobbled home.

"A few stitches at the ER and some Tylenol, and you'll be as good as new," Mom encouraged me. But when I woke up the next morning, I couldn't bend my leg—it was red, swollen, and throbbing, so back to the hospital we went.

The doctor popped one stitch open and whitish-yellow pus came oozing out. In less than twenty-four hours, infection had set in and was quickly spreading. By the time everything was said and done, I had a five-inch incision and twenty-six stitches down the back of my leg. But the original silver dollar-sized wound had to be left open so the pus could drain. It needed to heal from the inside out, the doctor said.

Twice a day for several weeks, I had to change the dressing, soaking gauze in saline solution and adding antibiotic ointment before stuffing it in the wound. I winced and grimaced as the medicine did its healing work, killing the bacteria and germs. As I think about it, these memories still give me the willies!

Today, I've got a pretty cool scar, like a salamander crawling up the back of my leg, but my body didn't heal overnight, and it didn't heal without the expert care of a doctor. Imagine how things might've ended differently if I grabbed a few Band-Aids and tried to bravely soldier on as infection spread throughout my body. Sure, I could have shrugged it off for a little while—taken a few more Tylenol and put on a happy face—but eventually I would've lost my leg or worse.

In one way or another, we've all been wounded by life in this broken world. Maybe it was a spear of our own making—sin that we willfully chose—or perhaps it was pain perpetrated by someone we trusted. A parent or spouse who walked out. A friend who betrayed us. A bully who made life miserable. A co-worker who spread lies. An abuser who took our innocence.

When our hearts are gashed open and bleeding, it's easy to numb the pain with virtual Tylenol—we work harder, eat more, lose ourselves in TV, or run up credit card bills for things we don't really need. We buy bigger toys, go on fancier vacations, reach for yet another drink, or surf the Internet for porn. We pursue pleasure any way we can in the hopes of healing ourselves.

But we can't. The infection spreads. "Your wound is incurable, your injury beyond healing" (JER. 30:12). The situation looks grim — no, impossible — and Satan looks on with glee as yet another warrior limps off the battlefield, stripped of any spiritual power.

In a culture that values strength and independence, it's tough to admit we are weak, broken, and in need of healing. Our enemy works overtime to cripple us with shame, guilt, and self-condemnation — to make us run away from God like Adam and Eve did, rather than straight into his loving arms. But Jesus Christ, our Great Physician, welcomes us to come exactly as we are — pus, infection, sin, and all — to bring our pain into the light of his presence and a safe community of believers.

The same way as my leg, our soul wounds can only heal from the inside out.

SCARS IN THE MAKING

I love each one of my children — Lulu, Belle, Knox, Tess, and Piper — beyond words, and there is nothing — not the worst temper tantrum or the most defiant attitude — that can ever change that. As a father, it breaks my heart to think that my children would ever try to hide something from me for fear of how I might respond. Whether they feel threatened or scared, embarrassed or ashamed, Ashley and I strive to be a safe place where our kids know they are deeply loved and always heard.

Never is the desire to be close to our little ones more intense than when the tears are rolling down their faces. In these moments, I'm pulled toward Tess like a magnet. It's not duty to rescue Lulu or obligation to comfort Piper. I believe my gut-level desire to draw near echoes back to the very first Father, our Abba.

"Come here, sweetheart." I want to scoop Belle up in my arms and hold her tight. I ache to ease Knox's pain in any way I possibly can. "Just relax. Daddy's here. Daddy's gonna take care of you and clean you up." While I can kiss boo-boos and apply Superman Band-Aids, I do not have the power to heal.

God, however, does.

"Do not despair, dear heart, but come to the Lord with all your jagged wounds, black bruises, and running sores," Charles Spurgeon admonishes. "He alone can heal, and he delights to do it. It is our Lord's office to bind up the brokenhearted, and he is gloriously at home at it."1 God is not turned off by your messiness or disgusted by your wounds. His heart is moved with compassion and a zealous desire to make you whole—to transform your wounds into scars that tell a story of redemption and hope (2 COR. 1:3-4):

> Blessed be the God and Father of our Lord Jesus Christ, the Father of mercies and God of all comfort, who comforts us in all our affliction so that we will be able to comfort those who are in any affliction with the comfort with which we ourselves are comforted by God.

What exactly is this comfort? The Greek word here is *paraklésis,* which means "a calling near, summons to comfort, solace, and encouragement, to offer refreshment."2 What an invitation! And yet, how often do we hesitate? Next time you find yourself an utter wreck, remember that God is calling you to himself.

"Come to me," Jesus beckons, "all who labor and are heavy laden, and I will give you rest...I will restore health to you and your wounds I will heal" (MT. 11:28; JER. 30:17). **Nearness to God heals our soul wounds from the inside out**, which is why Satan works overtime to keep us cowering in shame and fear, imprisoned by self-hatred and condemnation, or puffed up in pride and denial.

Did God really say he would heal you? Satan whispers. *Look at your life—it's a mess. I don't see any redemption. You're too far-gone, so you might as well stop fighting.*

Our spiritual enemy will do anything and everything in his power to keep us blind to the truth that "by [Jesus'] wounds we are healed" (IS. 53:5). This is not just a hope for heaven one day, but also a spiritual reality for today, right now, this moment. Jesus' death and resurrection 2,000 years ago undid the curse once and for all in the spiritual realm, but God's restorative work in our hearts and lives is an ongoing process that requires vulnerability, honesty, and daily pursuit.

Soul healing is not like microwaveable popcorn or instant coffee. It takes time, more like my daily wound dressings than a TV dinner. Caterpillars don't transform into butterflies in an instant, nor do tadpoles sprout legs overnight. Tomatoes take time to ripen, and roses don't blossom in an afternoon. The process of change and growth is woven into the fiber of all that God has created, including us.

It's drawing near to God even when we don't feel worthy, pressing into his grace when our hearts condemn us, and soaking our souls in the reality of who we are as his beloved sons and daughters. It's leaning into the pain of growth when the truth stings, letting go of our need for revenge, and surrendering our fears, dreams, and desires to God. It's "forgiv[ing] those who loved you poorly, step[ping] over your feelings of being rejected, and hav[ing] courage to trust that you won't fall into the abyss of nothingness but into the safe embrace of a God whose love will heal all your wounds," Henri Nouwen writes.[3]

Healing takes courage. Faith. Obedience. Patience. Prayer.

We witness examples in Scripture of Jesus suspending this natural order of things, healing a blind man or a leper in an instant. But this seems to be the exception, not the rule (although I will never cease to ask God in prayer for the exception!). Could it be that the faith we develop by walking out the journey of healing with God moment by moment would make a one-time miracle pale in comparison?

Your wounds are scars in the making—scars that will testify to the power of grace—but healing never happens in isolation.

FIGHTING THE GOOD FIGHT...TOGETHER

"Church is not an organization you join," Nicky Gumbel reflects, "it is a family where you belong, a home where you are loved, and a hospital where you find healing."[4] In this journey of becoming a dangerous Christian, walking together with our brothers and sisters in Christ is essential. God alone has the power to mend our broken hearts and heal our wounds, to rebuild our lives and restore our spiritual strength, but he often uses the Body of Christ as a catalyst.

At every juncture, Satan is looking for a chink in our armor, for a way to shut down the Holy Spirit's transformative work. I wonder how often we — perhaps even unknowingly — resist the work of Jesus in our hearts through playing into the devil's schemes?

Pride always stands in the way of healing. How easy it is to hold God and others at arms' length, convincing ourselves that we're not really *that* bad off. Recognizing our wounds and seeking help starts with admitting that we're spiritually bankrupt. We don't need self-improvement; we need redemption. It's the difference between the religious man's prayer, "God, I thank you that I am not like other people — robbers, evildoers, adulterers," and the tax collector's desperate plea, "God, have mercy on me, a sinner" (LK. 18:11-13). The hinge pin of healing is the devastating power of humility.

If Satan can't nab you with pride, he'll attack your heart with fear and self-preservation. Especially when we've been wounded by someone close to us — someone we trusted to protect and be there for us — it's easy to put up a wall, vowing, *I will never open myself up like that to get hurt again.* The devil's goal is to isolate and destroy. While wisdom is needed in identifying safe people to confide in, dismissing relationships all together will leave you fighting solo. You are not strong enough to fight temptation on your own — you won't last long.

Coming clean with our wounds and weaknesses — not just to God, but also with others — often triggers shame and self-hatred. Satan will have a heyday with your insecurities. *If these so-called friends of yours really knew the sick secrets you carry, they would drop you in an instant,* he taunts. *You are so filthy. You're an embarrassment to humanity, a disgrace, and a fraud.* And so we lie. We minimize. We ask for prayer about the deadline at work or the grandparent with health problems, but we fail to mention our relationship that's teetering on the edge of divorce.

The addiction we're struggling with.

The abuse we've suffered that haunts us every day.

The hopelessness that grips our hearts and leaves us contemplating suicide.

The sin that holds us captive.

The doubts about God that are tearing our faith to shreds.

The truth of the gospel offers a different path: "Therefore, there is now no condemnation for those who are in Christ Jesus" (ROM. 8:1). No need to pull out a Bible commentary here. No condemnation means just that—no condemnation. There is no shame at the foot of the Cross. This is the backdrop against which we are exhorted, "Confess your sins to each other and pray for each other so that you may be healed" (JAS. 5:16).

In the trenches of healing and recovery, we need comrades who are willing to fight alongside of us. We need witnesses to our pain—people who won't try to "fix" us, but who will listen, really listen, rather than offering cliché answers. Friends who will grieve deeply with us in the midst of loss, when we are faced head-on with the pain and evil of this fallen world. We need men and women who will embody grace to us—safe spaces where we can speak out our deepest sins and fears and hear the words, "I love you. I'm with you. Let's fight this together."

Living in community with other believers is not just a nice idea. It's more than potlucks and small groups and Sunday gatherings. It's going to war on behalf of each other in battles against lust and pornography, gossip and selfishness, people-pleasing and fear and greed. When we're wounded and weak and tempted to give up, it's standing in the gap, dismantling Satan's lies, and speaking truth and hope. Fellowship is woven into the heart and soul of our faith. It's a commitment to our brothers' and sisters' spiritual wellbeing. "Christianity was not meant to be lived individualistically," Daniel Darling writes. "When you put your faith in Christ, you are baptized into a Body, joined to a people."[5]

Are you joined to a people—or do you just attend a service on Sunday? The journey of living dangerously as a follower of Jesus is not for the faint of heart. The battle is not just out there—one day when we're healed and fit and ready to engage the enemy. The battle is here, right now, today. Turning wounds into weapons is warfare, because Satan knows what's at stake. He knows the power of your story to bring hope and transformation, to call others out of darkness and into the marvelous light of grace and forgiveness.

Our enemy will pull out all the stops to muzzle your voice, "But if we walk in the light, as he is in the light, we have fellowship with one another, and the blood of Jesus, his Son, purifies us from all sin" (1 JN. 1:7).

WEAPON POTENTIAL

Rather than strutting around tailgate parties bare-chested, I spend my energy these days trying to keep up with the 300-some elementary school kids here at Kanakuk each camp session. I love it. I wouldn't trade the world for the opportunity to serve and lead our amazing staff and campers. And while I often don crazy costumes of various sorts, my size twenty-five clown shoes and red cape have lost their appeal.

Its crazy, really—me, the guy who used to brag about how many beers I could drink, who rarely made it through a day without watching porn, who used other people to meet my own needs—now gets to boldly declare the truth that God can take any life and transform it for his glory. This is the heart of redemption, and Henri Nouwen suggests we each have a critical role to play in telling God's story:

> Nobody escapes being wounded. We are all wounded people, whether physically, emotionally, mentally, or spiritually. The main question is not, 'How can we hide our wounds?' so we don't have to be embarrassed, but 'How can we put our woundedness in the service of others?' When our wounds cease to be a source of shame, and become a source of healing, we have become wounded healers.[6]

In the hands of God, your greatest wound can become your greatest spiritual weapon. This book was birthed out of the sins, failures, and mistakes in my own story. Jesus puts these scars on display to testify to his promise that, "If you return, then I will restore you—before me you will stand; and if you extract the precious from the worthless, you will become my spokesman" (JER. 15:19, NASB).

God has transformed this brash and haughty Cyclone Commander into a follower of Jesus. The healing I have found in Christ is an unending source of passion and boldness. Having pursued all the pleasure this world has to offer and come up empty, I am jealous for others to experience the freedom, intimacy, and excitement of walking closely with Christ.

I've been forgiven of my sin, but there are still consequences. Memories haunt me of things I'm ashamed of, but as I continue to mature in my faith, these memories serve as the driving force that fuels my passion to help others get free. Satan knows my weak spots, but when he comes at me with temptation, his attacks only strengthen my resolve to break the silence and allow God to use my wounds to heal others.

What about you? What are the potential weapons in your life, perhaps long-buried in shame and fear, that God wants to unearth in service for his kingdom? When we live with a keen remembrance of where we've come from, we can never become puffed up at how God works through us. "Christianity is one beggar telling another beggar where he found bread," D.T. NILES writes.[7] It's not about being holier than thou; it's about being ruthlessly honest.

I have a seething hatred for addiction in its many forms — pornography, drugs, and alcohol to name a few. In my own life, these behaviors were my best attempts to numb the overwhelming pain I carried, to satisfy my heart with anything and everything but God. I get angry when I see my brothers and sisters taken captive. I've lived that lifestyle — been there, done that — and I know from experience that it never satisfies, that God's commands are for our good. I fight back by speaking openly about my failures, exposing the devil's lies for the empty sham they are.

In my personal journey of transformation, the desires of my heart have changed — what I once lived for now disgusts me. I'm not foolish enough to think I can't fall, but I have a sober confidence that these things do not own me. "Do not give the devil a foothold," Scripture challenges us (EPH. 4:27). "So I say, walk by the Spirit, and you will not gratify the desires of the flesh" (GAL. 5:16).

Here's the thing: **we are only dangerous when we are in Christ, for it is his power that emboldens us**. If we stray from his presence and the accountability of Christian community, relying on our own strength or wisdom, we open ourselves up to spiritual attack, for our old wounds to be re-infected.

What people and experiences, environments and activities in your life have the potential to draw you away from intimacy with God? It may not even be sin per say, but where is it leading you? "So, if you think you are standing firm, be careful that you don't fall!" (1 COR. 10:12). Walking out the journey of dangerous Christianity requires that we deal ruthlessly with anything that leads us toward pride and self-reliance. The battle isn't won or lost when you pull up the Internet browser or open the keg, but rather, when you start trusting your own ability to fight temptation rather than casting yourself each day at the feet of Jesus.

Toward the end of his life, Henri Nouwen looked back on his own personal dragons, realizing, "What once seemed such a curse has become a blessing. All the agony that threatened to destroy my life now seems like the fertile ground for greater trust, stronger hope, and deeper love."[8]

By stepping out with courage to face your brokenness, you open your heart up to experience God like never before, and more than that, to be on the front lines of his special forces, pushing back darkness in the exact sector where you were once captive. What formerly wreaked havoc in your life can be redeemed as an integral part of the adventure you share with God and the ministry he calls you to.

I can't think of a better example than my buddy Sam.

NOTHING IS WASTED

A few years ago, I was recruiting for summer camp staff at my alma mater, Iowa State, when Sam came bee-bopping up to the Kanakuk Kamps booth. A freshman, Sam had a big grin on his face and a twinkle in his eye. One of the joys of my job is getting to hear countless stories of God at work, and Sam's was no exception. Two years before, as he was heading into his senior year of high school, Sam's dad died of cancer. He wasn't there to help Sam move into the dorm, welcome him home for Christmas break, or dream together about the future.

With tears in his eyes, Sam shared with me the gaping hole his dad's passing left in his life, how he struggled to press in to God's presence in the midst of his grief. "You know what, though?" Sam reflected. "As terrible and gut-wrenching as these past few years have been, I wouldn't go back and change it because of what God has done in my life as a result."

Sam's faith challenged me. He went on to recount the holy upheaval that had taken place in the wake of his dad's death. Grappling with the brevity of life and what really mattered in the end gave Sam boldness to walk out his faith on a campus where many of his classmates could care less about God, or worse, actively made fun of Christians.

"Sam, I am so proud of you," I encouraged him. "You received a horrific wound in losing your dad, and yet, you've allowed Jesus to transform you — to turn that wound into a weapon for the gospel."

We had a great conversation, and I told Sam I couldn't wait to have him as part of our camp staff that summer. Walking out of the Union, Sam passed another student who was headed my direction. Carlie's face was downcast and it seemed her heart was heavy. She didn't have her application complete, and I was tempted to just tell her to mail it in, so we could do a phone interview. That way, I could get started packing up and head home to Ashley and the kiddos.

But I could feel the weight of her sadness, and the Holy Spirit stirred my heart to slow down, put the brakes on Shay's plans, and be present in the moment.

Carlie began to tear up as she told me that her dad had died four years ago from cancer. "I just can't seem to get back on my feet. I don't understand why God would take him away from me ...he was my best friend. I love God. He just doesn't feel present in my life."

As I listened, the Holy Spirit screamed in my soul, *Sam!*

"Do you happen to know the young man who walked out of here as you came in?" I asked Carlie.

"Yeah, that's Sam. I don't know him very well, but he lives on my hall," she responded nonchalantly. "Why?"

My heart beat faster. *What are the chances—out of 35,000 students—that Sam and Carlie live in the same dorm?*

"I know this is crazy, but would you mind if I call Sam? I think you two need to talk." She agreed, so I pulled out my phone. Sam answered from the line at Panda Express.

"Sam, get over here!" I could hardly contain my excitement. "I think God is about to do something big."

Sam abandoned ship on lunch and sat down to share his story with Carlie. At nineteen, with no ministry training, Sam began to minister to this wounded young woman in a way that I never could.

Sitting across from Sam in the Memorial Union that day, I saw a dangerous Christian. God had placed a weapon in Sam's hands and trained him to engage skillfully in a battle where human hearts are at their weakest—in the wake of tragedy and loss.

Sam didn't read a book or take a class to learn to wield this weapon—he lived it. He suffered deep wounds in the battlefield of loss. His daddy is gone. But rather than letting this tragedy cripple him with anger and bitterness, Sam made the courageous choice to run to Jesus in the midst of his anguish and pain, to rest in the arms of his Heavenly Father as he grieved, and something miraculous happened. Not overnight or in a flash from heaven, but the God of the Universe began to breathe new life into Sam's aching soul, to heal him from the inside out.

God not only gave Sam hope; he made him a warrior. This young man's scars testify that when someone you love is ripped out of your life, God is still there.

Sam has become a major problem for the enemy. Satan's attacks are defenseless against the weapon of Sam's redemptive story—and yours, too. Nothing is wasted. Whatever you have experienced in your life—whatever tragedy you've walked through, what-ever mistakes you've made and consequences you've suffered as a result—Jesus wants to take what the enemy intends for evil and fashion it into a weapon for good. There are no exceptions here. Maybe you feel like you're one big festering wound and you've all but given up hope.

I beg you, don't. Don't let shame and self-condemnation win.
There is no sin too great and no loss too tragic, no life circumstance too messy that God's love cannot conquer, heal, and transform it. You and I have a calling, N.T. WRIGHT reminds us:

> Our task as image-bearing, God-loving, Christ-shaped, Spirit-filled Christians, following Christ and shaping our world, is to announce redemption to a world that has dicovered its fallenness, to announce healing to a world that has discovered its brokenness, to proclaim love and trust to a world that knows only exploitation, fear, and suspicion. [9]

God longs to heal you from the inside out, birthing his calling for you as a dangerous Christian out of your greatest failures and losses. So don't try to tough it out or ignore the pain in your soul. Hobble, walk, crawl—however you get there, bring your wounds to Jesus, and he'll forge a story of hope that will make the devil tremble.

The God of the Universe will empower you to run.

CHAPTER TWELVE

RUN

Before the sleepy, lukewarm, faithless, namby-pamby Christian world, we will dare to trust our God, we will venture our all for him, we will live and die for him, and we will do it with his joy unspeakable singing aloud in our hearts.
— *C. T. Studd*

By nature, I'm a pretty slow runner, but in college, I started to jog a mile as part of my regular workout. The first day, I was out of breath after two laps around the track, but as time went on, my endurance grew.

One mile turned to two, two turned to three, and one day I surprised myself by running five miles. *I wonder if I could run a marathon?* I dreamed. The following Sunday, after a sizeable lunch, I decided to go for a jog.

Mile one — check.

Mile two — hit the dust.

You know what? I'm feeling pretty good. I'm in decent shape. Forget training — I think I can run a marathon today! I thought a bit arrogantly.

Eight miles in — the furthest I had ever run in my life — and I was flying along. My confidence was through the roof.

At mile twelve, I tried to shake nagging pain in my lower back. It felt like someone was wrenching my kidneys. Turns out, when you get dehydrated, your kidneys are one of the first organs to shut down. Soon, my whole body began to lock up. I was disoriented and so desperate for water that I ran into people's front yards and started sucking on their water hoses for a drink.

The will to survive eventually overruled my pride, and I realized I had better turn back so Ashley didn't find me on the side of the road. I hobbled home, discouraged and delirious with pain. I managed to make it barely fifteen miles — well short of my intended goal.

I realized you can't just stumble into running a marathon — zeal, passion and willpower aren't enough. Long-distance running requires discipline, training, and a daily commitment.

That day, I decided to stop showing off and really get serious about running. The Music City Marathon in Nashville was coming up in a few months, so I signed up before I could talk myself out of it.

I don't care how grueling the training is or how many hours I have to put in, I vowed. I am going to cross that finish line in Nashville.

Despite what the Nike and Reebok commercials would have you believe, training isn't all that glamorous. After doing one of my long runs, I limped up to our house and fell through the doorway. Lying there with half of my body in the living room and the other half on the front porch, the voice of doubt was loud and clear: *There is no way you'll ever make it. Seventeen miles and you're about to die? A marathon is nine more than that!*

Race day came, and I showed up at the crack of dawn with 30,000 of my best friends. I cruised through the first ten miles — no sweat. Some pretty intense leg cramps set in, but I refused to slow down. I made it to mile nineteen and faced a tortuous hill ahead.

That's when I hit the wall. Every muscle, bone, and ligament in my body screamed, "Stop, Shay! Stop, or you're gonna die!"

Three months of training had made me stubborn, though. A swig of Gatorade at the aid station revived me a bit. I tuned out the pain as best as I could and did the only thing I knew to do: put one foot in front of the other.

But nothing could have prepared me for the second wall. By mile twenty-three, I was ready to crawl off the course and right into an ambulance gurney! I was reduced to the emotional state of a toddler. I would have broken down sobbing, only my body didn't have enough moisture left to eke out a tear.

My feet went completely numb, which left me "nubbing" along—hobbling as if on the two stumps of my legs. With each step, it felt like nails were being driven up through the very feet I couldn't feel. Racers were passing me left and right, but at this point, I didn't even care.

"Way to go, man! You're almost there!" I looked over to see a guy sitting on his motorcycle and desperately wanted to ask him for a ride to the finish line.

"How far is it?" I mustered up the energy to form the words.

"A half a mile, man. You're almost there!"

My heart dropped into my stomach—at that point in my life, a half-mile seemed like an insurmountable distance! Limping along and certain that the next step would be my last, I was in a total daze.

Crowds lined the course, cheering their brains out. Runners were grabbing their pregnant wives, their grannies, and their kids out of the crowd to cross the finish line with them. Music pumped over the loudspeakers as an emcee announced names and finishing times in dramatic fashion. People were smiling, laughing, posing for pictures, and breaking into celebratory dance.

Me? I was in shock. I couldn't believe I had actually crossed the finish line in one piece.

Ultimately, that marathon didn't begin with the shot of a pistol. **It started months before when I made the heart decision to be "all in."** To keep training, keep running, and keep putting one foot in front of the other no matter what obstacles I faced.

Living as a dangerous Christian is no different. You can't try it out like a free month on Netflix or a new workout routine. You can't add it to your calendar or tack it on to your already-busy life. You have to abandon everything and jump in with both feet. Otherwise, when you hit a wall of suffering or spiritual attack, what will keep you going?

WHAT THE TORTOISE AND THE HARE GOT ALL WRONG

Some people approach the Christian life a lot like the tortoise in Aesop's fable. "Don't push yourself too hard for God," they say.

"After all, this is a marathon, not a hundred-meter dash. Take your time. Run at a pace that feels good and is comfortable for you. You know—slow and steady wins the race. And make sure you have some fun along the way."

Growing up in a Christian home, I figured that I would really start following Jesus as a teenager. After all, God couldn't expect too much from a kid, right?

In high school, I got distracted with parties and girls and being cool, but I convinced myself, "Everybody's got to sow a few wild oats. I'll get serious about my faith when I go off to college."

College came and, well, you know the story there. "I'm having too much fun right now," I reasoned. "I'll get my act together when I graduate. I'll surrender my life to God then."

I took my first job in California and pushed back the timeline yet again. "I kinda just feel like doing whatever I want. (YOLO, right?) When I get married—that's when I'll settle down and really commit to this Christian life thing."

Ever been there? Satan uses this mindset to keep us weak, powerless, and self-consumed: *One day, I'll really get serious about following Jesus. But first, let me* _____.

I wonder…how do you fill in the blank with your decisions each day?

First let me enjoy college? Have a little fun? Travel the world? Find a spouse? Get out of debt? Build my career?

Real life isn't one day—it's today. Right now, as you read these words, Jesus is inviting you to follow him. To abandon everything you know and hold onto for comfort, security, and identity, and begin to live dangerously.

I don't know many soldiers who take a "slow and steady" approach to war. They train. They discipline themselves. They hone their senses and practice battle maneuvers over and over and over again, until it becomes second nature.

Maybe you're more like the hare, though, in Aesop's story. You're "all in" when it comes to following Jesus, and you set out on your life of faith much like I did trying to run a marathon after Sunday lunch. You're passionate—reckless even—and you will stop at nothing to advance God's kingdom. After all, better to burn out for God than rust out, right?

Whatever God is doing, you want to be on the front lines, but often, you go after the devil in your own strength. You pride yourself on all the amazing ways God is using you, making sure to showcase your ministry, your talents, and your battle-wins for the world to see. You wear your spiritual victories like a badge of honor.

It may look good, but at the end of the day, when we live like this, we're just as powerless as the tortoise, because pride and self-sufficiency always shut down the work of the Holy Spirit. In our own strength, we won't last more than a skirmish or two. One way or another, Satan will take you out. You cannot win God-sized battles with human strength.

Is there a better way? Paul thought so.

DITCHING THE STATUS QUO

"[I]n a race all the runners run, but only one gets the prize...Run in such a way as to get the prize," he writes (1 COR. 9:24). Some days, I wish I could sit down with Paul and pick his brain. *What's the secret, Paul? Teach me how to run!*

As a respected leader in the Jewish faith, Paul had a lot going for him. Money. Power. Fame. Influence. You name it. In today's lingo, he might say, "I graduated from an Ivy League school, my book is a New York Times bestseller, my online following is exploding, and I've been named one of the top ten influential leaders of the year."

Paul thought he was *the man*...until he met Jesus on the road to Damascus and caught a glimpse of this God-man who turned his life upside down. That day, Paul made a heart decision—he surrendered his life to Jesus, not just for the hope of heaven, but in order to engage with the battle right in front of him.

He decided to stop fighting Jesus and start fighting for him.

Living dangerously is not about pushing ourselves harder, doing more, or muscling our way through combat with Satan. In fact, it's just the opposite: "Put no confidence in the flesh," Paul admonishes (PHIL. 3:3).

He continues in Colossians 3:8-9:

I consider everything a loss because of the surpassing worth of knowing Christ Jesus my Lord, for whose sake I have lost all things. I consider them garbage, that I may gain Christ and be found in him, not having a righteousness of my own that comes from the law, but that which is through faith in Christ.

Running is ultimately about chasing after him—not ministry opportunities or spiritual battles. We pursue Jesus in the posture of humility. As we seek his face and sit in his presence, everyone and everything else that captured our attention and stirred our affection begins to pale in comparison.

It's worthless. Garbage. In fact, the Greek word Paul uses here, *skubalon*, actually means dung.[1] Sometimes the biggest barrier to living dangerously is ourselves—our pride, our need for approval, our desire to be noticed, accepted, and valued.

"Let all that go," Paul encourages us. "This journey isn't about you—your life, your dreams, your victories—it's about the life of Jesus flowing through you. It's about being faithful right where you are, pressing into Christ, walking in step with his Spirit."

I wonder, what's slowing you down in your pursuit of Jesus? What's holding you back? Is it really worth it? At the end of the day—when you lay your head down on your pillow at night—does it really satisfy?

Could it be Jesus is inviting you into a greater "yes" on the other side of surrender—of saying "no" to whatever person, behavior, activity, or environment has become your comfort zone?

"Let us throw off everything that hinders and the sin that so easily entangles. And let us run with perseverance the race marked out for us" (HEB. 12:1).

In this race of life, are you just trying to keep the pace with the people around you? Or are you setting trends, breaking records, and pursuing Jesus with every ounce of strength and energy you've got?

When I was training for my marathon, a friend introduced me to the concept of *negative splits*. It's one of the most gut-wrenching, muscle-searing, lactic-acid-producing training strategies out there, and yet, it's the key to finishing well.

Here's the gist of negative splits: run every lap faster than the one before. Tackle every mile with greater intensity, every hill with more determination than the last…until you cross the finish line. Don't slow down. Don't give up. Don't lose heart.

I can't think of a better illustration of what it looks like to chase after Jesus: pursuing him with greater passion today than you did yesterday. Being more ruthless against sin. Attacking Satan's lies with greater vengeance. Obeying the voice of his Spirit more quickly. Loving others more deeply. Opening your heart more generously. Taking back more spiritual ground from the enemy with each decision, each interaction, each moment.

Enough with the status quo! When we pace ourselves, we miss out on the power of God. Our broken world needs brave hearts. God is looking for trendsetters—men and women who will push back darkness every day as his kingdom is forcefully advancing (MT. 11:12).

WHEN YOU FALL

The year was 2008. The event, the women's 600-meter run at the Big Ten Indoor Track Championships. Headed into the final lap, Heather Dorniden was in the lead. One moment, she seemed invincible…the next, she was flat on her face, skidding along the track.

Maybe you can relate. If you're anything like me, you've made a lot of mistakes. The reality is that, "All have sinned and have fallen short of the glory of God" (ROM. 3:23). We're all fallible, broken people. We're going to fall…sometimes, daily.

I might've been tempted to crawl over to the sidelines, nurse my wounds, and call it a day. And nothing would make the devil happier than for you and I to get stuck in self-pity.

But not Heather. In an instant, she was back on her feet. The other contestants had left her in the dust, but she refused to let this trip-up define her run.

Heather gave it everything.

In less than thirty seconds, she passed not one…not two… but every single woman ahead of her. That day, defying all odds, Heather crossed the finish line first.[2]

In this race of the Christian life, the real question isn't whether or not you'll face plant at some point. Satan will do everything in his power to trip you up, and he'll disguise it in a million appealing ways. **When you fall, it's what you do next that matters most.**

Life is too short to stay angry, ashamed, addicted, apathetic, or anxious. It's too short to stay blind, fearful, embarrassed, or hardened. It's too short to stay lazy, to procrastinate, to be proud, selfish, or stubborn.

While others wallow in shame and condemnation, dangerous Christians fight back: "Resist the devil, and he will flee from you" (JAS. 4:7). The devil can taunt you and he can tempt you, he can whisper lies in your ear, but he has no power over your soul.

Press in to Jesus. Open wide your heart to his grace. There is forgiveness, healing, and restoration. Let every fall fuel your spiritual passion. Respond to failure in such a way that Satan will regret ever trying to mess with you. Remember, you aren't his prisoner anymore.

You are free...not to pursue your every whim and desire, but to run in the path of God's commands (PS. 119:32). Before the foundation of the world, the God of the Universe wrote into his grand story of redemption a plan and purpose for your life. He created you with unique gifts, talents, and personality traits. You have a pivotal role to play in this messy, beautiful, hope-filled journey of God restoring all things to himself.

"We are God's workmanship, created in Christ Jesus to do good works, which God prepared in advance for us to do" (EPH. 2:10). Your Heavenly Father is not waiting for you to be perfect or get your act together. He's not scrutinizing your every move to see if you "make the cut" to be part of his elite team. All he asks is that you come. Abandon everything you once held dear and chase after his heart, rather than happiness, self-satisfaction, or worldly success.

A few years ago, I came across the book *In the Dust of the Rabbi* by Ray Vander Laan. His big idea is this: when Jesus approached the disciples and invited them, "Follow me," he led them through the Judean wilderness—a dry and arid desert. The roads they traveled together were a far cry from our superhighways. They were winding, dusty trails.

These men walked so closely behind Jesus that the dust from his sandals settled on their clothes, their shoes, even their hair. Living life with Jesus changed them.[3] The Jewish Council was dumfounded: "When they saw the courage of Peter and John and realized that they were unschooled, ordinary men, they were astonished and they took note that these men had been with Jesus" (ACTS 4:13). I pray that may be said of us. But too often, I fear that we become self-absorbed and distracted. We mosey along at our own pace or dash off in thoughtless zeal. Even in our ministry pursuits, there may be little trace of the dust of the Rabbi.

Plain and simple, you and I are only as dangerous in the spiritual realm as we are connected with Christ. In Jesus, the same power that raised Jesus from the dead is at our fingertips. Take a minute to reflect on your life:

Are you on the sidelines, discouraged and ashamed after a fall?

Are you running in your own strength—pacing yourself for fear your energy will run out?

Or could it be that you're chasing after good things that God never called you to?

ONE SECOND AT A TIME

My buddy Keith Chancey never met a stranger in his life. Passing through Dallas on a trip, he struck up a conversation with a fellow customer at a restaurant.

A stocky guy with a gorilla grip, Brandon was built like a wrestler, but his personality was unassuming and down to earth. He didn't brag on himself one bit, and Keith had to keep probing to hear more about his story.

Turns out, Brandon wasn't just any wrestler. He was Brandon Slay—gold medalist at the 2000 Sydney Olympics!

Somehow, Keith convinced his new friend to show him the gold medal. They traveled across town to his humble apartment, and Brandon reached into the back of his sock drawer to retrieve the prize. Standing in the presence of a world-renowned athlete, Keith was amazed.

"How did you become the best in the world?" he asked.

"Well, good wrestlers break it down by the period," Brandon explained. "There are three periods in a wrestling match, so they adopt the mindset, *I'm going to give it everything I've got to win this period.*

"Great wrestlers break the match down by the minute—the next sixty seconds I'm going to give it everything I've got."

"I broke my matches down by the second. Walking onto the mat, I decided, *I'm going to give it everything I've got this second. And the next second. And the next second…all the way through to the final second of the third period.*"

This is a critical secret of dangerous Christianity: break the battle down — one second at a time — and exercise your victory in Christ in each moment. "Life is war," Paul Tripp writes. "It is being fought on the turf of your heart. It is fought for the control of your soul. Each situation you face today is a skirmish in the war."[4]

Every decision. Every encounter. Every moment matters.

When you're walking into class or your sorority house, the break room or the living room: *God, give me strength to make decisions that are pleasing to you. To speak and act in such a way that brings you glory. Show me how to love and serve the people around me.* When you get in a car accident or get a call from your kid's teacher or get in a fight with your spouse: *Lord, empower me to respond with grace and wisdom. Help me to be quick to listen and slow to speak. Open my eyes to see your perspective on this situation.*

When you're stressed out in a business meeting or angry at someone who's hurt you, lonely and surfing the Internet or scared about what the doctor might say: *Jesus, I need your Holy Spirit to be strong where I am weak. I can't overcome this challenge on my own.*

When Satan whispers, "No one will ever know. Just give in. Do what feels good."

These are the moments that make up our lives. They may not feel grand and glorious. After all, you likely won't hear the Braveheart soundtrack playing in the background, and if you go around swinging the Claymore—well, it might not end well.

But these are fighting moments. These ordinary circumstances are exactly where God wants to meet you—to empower you to stand firm against temptation and to equip you to take an offensive position against your enemy. Consider these words of Kaj Munk, a Danish pastor and playwright who was martyred by the Gestapo in 1944:

> *What is, therefore, our task today? Shall I answer: "Faith, hope, and love"? That sounds beautiful. But I would say — courage. No, even that is not challenging enough to be the whole truth. Our task today is recklessness. For what we Christians lack is not psychology or literature…we lack a holy rage — the recklessness which comes from the knowledge of God and humanity. The ability to rage when justice lies prostrate on the streets, and when the lie rages across the face of the earth…a holy anger about the things that are wrong in the world… To rage against complacency. To restlessly seek that recklessness that will challenge and seek to change human history until it conforms to the norms of the kingdom of God.*[5]

What is your battlefield? It's whatever is right in front of you. Whatever breaks your heart, whatever injustice eats you alive and makes you angry. Pay attention. God just may be stirring up bravery and a holy rage to engage in combat against the devil.

Why not ask him — *what do you have for me, Lord? How would you have me join you in bringing hope and redemption in this arena?*

IN PURSUIT OF ONE THING

Summers at Kanakuk Kamps are exhausting. I wouldn't trade the high-energy, never-ending excitement of camp for anything, but it's not always easy. Recently, though, I realized that I have more energy at thirty-five than I did as a camp counselor in my twenties.

What's the difference? It has been quite some time since I prayed for energy. These days, I pray for passion. It was passion that drove Jesus to the Cross. Passion enabled our Savior to envision "the joy set before him" in order to willingly take on incredible anguish and suffering so that we might be restored as beloved sons and daughters of God (HEB. 12:2).

Jesus is jealous for your affections. He doesn't just want your mental assent to his existence or a few hours of your time on

Sunday. His heart aches for you to lay aside guilt and shame, to cast off self-made religion and the need to earn his love—and live passionately.

Passion is birthed out of humility, and prayer is the conduit through which it flows. As we rest in God's grace and forgiveness and pursue intimacy with him, God offers us supernatural energy, strength, and spiritual power. In the words of the prophet Isaiah, "Those who hope in the Lord will renew their strength. They will soar on wings like eagles; they will run and not grow weary, they will walk and not be faint" (IS. 40:31).

This sort of godly passion is not something you can drum up on your own. It's the byproduct of having been with Jesus. And it's dangerous. Passion will change you. It will turn your world upside down and reorient your perspective and priorities. It may well lead you into suffering, and it will most certainly require you to die to yourself.

Godly passion moves mountains, demolishes strongholds, sets captives free, and breathes life into hopeless places. It will empower you to step boldly into our broken world each day with a brave heart and unshakeable faith.

Your family needs you. Your community needs you. The oppressed need you. The abused need you. The forgotten need you. However, God does not.

God doesn't need you. He wants you. He loves you...deeply.

And out of that love, he longs to entrust you with a key role in his redemptive plan. Your Heavenly Father wants to give you more than salvation. He has carved out a unique purpose that you have been created to fulfill. At the end of the day, only one thing matters, Paul reminds us: "Forgetting what is behind and straining forward to what is ahead, I press on toward the goal to win the prize for which God has called me heavenward in Christ Jesus" (PHIL. 3:14).

YOUR JOURNEY BEGINS...

Just days after the horrific events of September 11, 2001, Pastor Carter Conlon stood in front of his congregation in central Manhattan.

What could he say to offer hope as his city reeled in the wake of unspeakable tragedy? In the midst of chaos and confusion, Conlon called his church—and you and I today—to step out with passion and bravery like never before:

"We have got to lay our lives down for the purposes of God. This is not a Sunday school picnic—the church of Jesus Christ. This is not an invitation to have continuous good times. This is a war for the souls of men…It's not just about an opposing theology or conflicting viewpoint on Jesus. This is about your life…

"As people were fleeing from a crumbling building, there were police officers and firemen and others, that were running *towards* the building, saying, 'Run for your life!' at their own peril. And in many cases I believe they knew that they would die, but they knew that there was a sense of duty."

With renewed passion to chase after God, Conlon cried out, " 'Jesus, don't let my sense of duty be less for your kingdom than these beloved firemen and policemen were for those perishing in the falling tower.'

"We're living in a generation where truth is falling into the streets. I want to be among those that are not running away from the conflict, but running into the conflict, saying, 'Run for your life!' "6

In these chapters, we've pulled back the curtain and seen that "our struggle is not against flesh and blood, but against…the spiritual forces of evil in the heavenly realms" (EPH. 6:12).

And as this book comes to a close, your journey of living dangerously for the gospel is only just beginning. Struggle well, my friends. Pursue Christ with an undivided heart. When your feet hit the floor in the morning, purpose to run negative splits. May you have courage—no, recklessness—to engage valiantly in the strength of God.

Be faithful. Love radically. Refuse to accept the status quo. Partner with God in "rescu[ing] those being led away to death" (PROV. 24:11). Push back darkness with the light of the gospel in your little corner of this world.

Say "yes" to the Holy Spirit—one moment at a time—until we gather around God's throne and the war is finally over.

HOW HAS DANGEROUS CHRISTIAN
IMPACTED YOUR LIFE?

We'd love to hear how you're #livingdangerously in your corner of the world and the #dangerouschristian that is an example to you!

Join the conversation on Facebook @Dangerous Christian book, Twitter @d_c_book, or Instagram @dangerouschristian.

ACKNOWLEDGMENTS

I owe many thanks in the wake of this project. In some ways, I feel like I have contributed the least because of the generosity and skill of everyone involved. First and foremost, I am grateful to God for forgiveness, redemption, and the message of this book. I am honored to carry the banner of Jesus Christ, and to push back spiritual darkness through these pages.

A huge thanks to my wife, Ashley, who has loved and believed in me no matter what. Dangerous Christian represents a big risk for our family, but Ashley has always encouraged me to swing for the fences. She is perfectly suited for me...I am so blessed. Thank you to the many influencers who have shaped me, starting with my parents, Rob and Susan Robbins, who laid the foundation of faith. And thanks to God for sending reinforcements—including Shawn Peterson, Keith Chancey, Ted Cunningham, Ward Wiebe and most of all, Joe White. I am so humbled to be surrounded by such godly men as I stumble toward Jesus each day. They have picked me up and set me back on course more times than I can count.

I also want to thank the Dangerous Christian team. God has blessed me with incredibly talented friends! We have built a publishing company from scratch and I would put their skill set up against any team in the country. Thanks to my co-author, Laura Captari, who has taken my dream and made it a work of art. Her skill, professionalism, and patience have touched every word. I'm eternally indebted to my thorough and skilled editing team: David Marvin, Joey Tisdale, and Aubrey Ellett from Watermark Church; Brad Mooney from the Kanakuk Institute; Lindsay Rother from Kanakuk Kamps; and precious friends Jason and Katie Robinson and Bob Schuchardt. Thank you for taking time to read, pray over, and give feedback on the manuscript.

Thanks are also in order to Brandon Butcher for his design, branding, and friendship, and to Bill Chlanda for the phenomenal layout. Big props go to Derek Nassick for building a killer marketing strategy, and to our grassroots marketing team for helping to get the word out.

Every heart emboldened through these pages wouldn't have happened without each of you. What a team!

ABOUT THE AUTHORS

SHAY ROBBINS is a follower of Jesus Christ. He is the proud husband of Ashley Robbins. Together they have five awesome kiddos. Shay is a graduate of Iowa State University and the Kanakuk Institute. He is a Director at Kanakuk Kamps, a Christian sports camp in southern Missouri. Shay is also a member of the teaching team at Woodland Hills Family Church. He is the founder of LifeEcho.com, a social media application designed to connect, equip and multiply discipleship relationships. Shay is a passionate and gifted communicator. If you are interested in having him speak at your church or organization, or if you'd like to share how Dangerous Christian has impacted your life, he'd love to hear from you at dangerouschristian@gmail.com.

Web: www.dangerouschristian.com
Facebook: Dangerous Christian book
Twitter: @d_c_book
Instagram: @dangerouschristian

LAURA CAPTARI is a follower of Jesus, lover of stories, and coffee fanatic. She is the co-author of multiple books, including Dangerous Christian, Face to Face, and Orphan Justice. Laura previously served on staff with the American Association of Christian Counselors and is currently a doctoral student at the University of North Texas, where she researches the role of faith and safe community in building resilience and post-traumatic growth following trauma, disaster, and loss. A psychologist in training, she is passionate about helping others find healing from trauma and loss. Laura is an avid traveler and runner, and seeks to approach each day as a new adventure in grace.

NOTES

Chapter 2: The Devastating Power of Humility
[1]John Eldredge, *The Sacred Romance: Drawing Closer to the Heart of God* (Nashville, TN: Thomas Nelson, 1997), 232.
[2]C.S. Lewis, *The Weight of Glory* (New York: HarperCollins, 1976), 26.
[3]"Luó," *Biblehub.com,* accessed August 1, 2016, http://biblehub.com/greek/3089.htm.
[4]"Endunamoó," *Biblehub.com,* accessed August 1, 2016, http://biblehub.com/greek/1743.htm.
[5]Tim Keller, *Counterfeit Gods: The Empty Promises of Money, Sex, and Power, and the Only Hope That Matters* (New York: Penguin Group, 2009), 88.
[6]Reverend L. Tyerman, *The Life and Times of the Rev. John Wesley, M.A., Founder of the Methodists* (London: Hodder and Stoughton, 1871).
[7]Martin Luther, quoted in Patrick Morley, *A Man's Guide to the Spiritual Disciplines: 12 Habits to Strengthen Your Walk with Christ* (Chicago, IL: Moody, 2007), 55.
[8]Elizabeth Howell, "How Many Stars are in the Universe?", *Space.com,* May 31, 2014, http://www.space.com/26078-how-many-stars-are-there.html.
[9]Rose Eveleth, "There are 37.2 Trillion Cells in Your Body," *Smithsonian.com,* October 24, 2013, http://www.smithsonianmag.com/smart-news/there-are-372-trillion-cells-in-your-body-4941473/?no-ist.

Chapter 3: Forgiven and Set Free
[1]"Teleó," *Biblehub.com,* accessed August 1, 2016, http://biblehub.com/greek/5055.htm.
[2]"Splagchnizomai," *Biblehub.com,* accessed August 1, 2016, http://biblehub.com/greek/4697.htm.
[3]Charles Stanley, quoted in Lance Colkmire, ed., *Evangelical Sunday School Lesson Commentary* 2013-2014 (Cleveland, TN: Pathway Press, 2013), 131.
[4]Henri Nouwen, *The Return of the Prodigal Son* (New York: Doubleday, 1992), 43.
[5]Tim Keller with Kathy Keller, *The Meaning of Marriage: Facing the Complexities of Commitment with the Wisdom of God* (New York: Dutton, 2011), 19.
[6]Matt Chandler, "Forgiveness," Sermon, *The Village Church,* Flower Mound, TX, December 9, 2012, http://thevillagechurch.net/resources/sermons/detail/forgiveness/.
[7]Martin Luther, *Luther's Works, Volume 31: Career of the Reformer I,* ed. Harold J. Grim and Helmut T. Lehmann (Philadelphia, PA: Fortress Press, 1957), 25.
[8]Ibid., 53.

[9]Corrie ten Boom, *The Hiding Place* (New York: Bantam, 1971), 271.
[10]Corrie ten Boom, "I'm Still Learning to Forgive," *Guideposts* (Carmel, NY: Guideposts Associates, Inc., 1972), https://www.guideposts.org/inspiration/stories-of-hope/guideposts-classics-corrie-ten-boom-on-forgiveness?nopaging=1.
[11]Ibid.
[12]Ibid.
[13]Ibid.
[14]Alan Redpath, "58 Alan Redpath Quotes," *Christianquotes.info,* accessed August 1, 2016, http://www.christianquotes.info/quotes-by-author/alan-redpath-quotes/.

Chapter 4: The Sword of the Spirit
[1]"Dabaq," *Biblehub.com,* accessed August 1, 2016, http://biblehub.com/hebrew/1692.htm.
[2]"Logos," *Biblehub.com,* accessed August 1, 2016,http://biblehub.com/greek/3056.htm.
[3]A.W. Tozer, *The Pursuit of God* (Ventura, CA: Regal, 2013), 72.
[4]Michael Horton, quoted in Bill Bradfield, ed., *On Reading the Bible: Thoughts and Reflections of Over 500 Men and Women,* from St. Augustine to Oprah Winfrey (Mineola, NY: 2005), 57.
[5]James Merritt, quoted in Stephen Kyeyune, *The New Generation of Worshipers in the 21st Century* (Bloomington, IN: AuthorHouse, 2012), 138.
[6]Saint Augustine, "Augustine Quote—Letters from Home," *Christianquotes. info,* accessed August 1, 2016, http://www.christianquotes.info/images/augustine-quote-letters-from-home/.
[7]Søren Kierkegaard, quoted in Bernard Ramm, *Protestant Biblical Interpretation* (Grand Rapids, MI: Baker, 1999), 75.
[8]"Rhéma," *Biblehub.com,* accessed August 1, 2016, http://biblehub.com/greek/4487.htm.
[9]Brother Yun and Paul Hattaway, *The Heavenly Man: The Remarkable True Story of Chinese Christian Brother Yun* (Grand Rapids, MI: Kregel Publications, 2002).
[10]Napoleon Bonaparte, quoted in Michael Shea, "Napoleon Bonaparte—On the Divinity of Jesus Christ, at Saint Helena—1820," *Godtheoriginalintent.com,* accessed August 1, 2016, http://www.godtheoriginalintent.com/PDF%20Chapters/Napoleon%20Bonaparte.pdf.

Chapter 5: Seeking God
[1]"Darash," *Biblehub.com,* accessed August 1, 2016, http://biblehub.com/hebrew/1875.htm.
[2]Hannah Hurnard, *Hinds' Feet on High Places* (Shippensburg, PA: Destiny Image, 2005), 44.
[3]"Towb," *Biblehub.com,* accessed August 1, 2016, http://biblehub.com/hebrew/2896.htm.
[4]C.S. Lewis, *The Last Battle* (New York: HarperCollins, 2005), 196.

[5] *August Rush*, directed by Kirsten Sheridan (Burbank, CA: Warner Home Video, 2007), DVD.

[6] "Proseché," *Biblehub.com*, accessed August 1, 2016, http://biblehub.com/greek/4337.htm.

[7] Brother Lawrence, *The Practice of the Presence of God* (New Kensington, PA: Whitaker House, 1982), 35, 62.

[8] Richard Foster, *Celebration of Discipline: The Path to Spiritual Growth* (New York: HarperOne, 1998).

[9] Fred Ward, "The History of Pearls," *PBS.org*, accessed August 1, 2016, http://www.pbs.org/wgbh/nova/ancient/history-pearls.html.

Chapter 6: Hearing God

[1] Aaron Smith, "Americans and Text Messaging," *Pew Research Center*, September 19, 2011, http://www.pewinternet.org/2011/09/19/americans-and-text-messaging/; "52 Percent Of Consumers Prefer Text Conversations with Support Reps Over Their Current Support Method," Business Wire, April 2, 2014, http://www.businesswire.com/news/home/20140402005509/en/52-Percent-Consumers-Prefer-Text-Conversations-Support.

[2] Aaron Smith, "Americans and Text Messaging," *Pew Research Center*, September 19, 2011, http://www.pewinternet.org/2011/09/19/americans-and-text-messaging/.

[3] Albert Mehrabian, *Nonverbal Communication* (New Brunswick: Aldine Transaction, 1972).

[4] John Piper, Sermon, *Linger Conference*, Watermark Church, Dallas, Texas, February 14-15, 2014.

[5] George Müller and W. Elfe Tayler, *Passages from the Diary and Letters of Henry Craik of Bristol* (London: J.F. Shaw & Co., 1866), xii.

[6] Oswald Chambers, "Do Not Quench the Spirit," *Utmost.org*, accessed August 1, 2016, https://utmost.org/do-not-quench-the-spirit//.

[7] Saint Augustine, quoted in John Bevere, Good or God: *Why Good without God Isn't Enough* (Palmer Lake, CO: Messenger Intl., 2015), 89.

Chapter 7: The Weapon of Prayer

[1] Jack Wellman, "Who Was Leonard Ravenhill?" *Patheos.com*, June 15, 2016, http://www.patheos.com/blogs/christiancrier/2016/06/15/who-was-leonard-ravenhill/.

[2] Leonard Ravenhill, "Quotes," *Leonard-ravenhill.com*, accessed August 1, 2016, http://www.leonard-ravenhill.com/quotes.

[3] Ibid.

[4] Leonard Ravenhill, "Quotes of Leonard Ravenhill," *Gospeltruth.net*, accessed August 1, 2016, http://www.gospeltruth.net/ravenhill.htm.

[5] A.B. Simpson, "The Pattern Prayer," *Worldinvisible.com*, accessed August 1, 2016, http://www.worldinvisible.com/library/simpson/5b00.0148/5b00.0148.01.htm.

[6] Sadhu Sundar Singh, quoted in Nick Harrison, *Magnificent Prayer: 366 Devotions to Deepen Your Prayer Experience* (Grand Rapids, MI: Zondervan, 2010), 218.

7"Energéō," *Biblehub.com,* accessed August 1, 2016, http://biblehub.com/greek/1754.htm.

Chapter 8: Daily Bread

1Abraham Lincoln, quoted in Hendry Mills Alden and Thomas Bucklin Wells, eds., *Harper's Magazine, Volume 31* (New York: Harper, 1865), 226.

2"Ptóchos," *Biblehub.com,* accessed August 1, 2016, http://biblehub.com/greek/4434.htm.

3Ibid.

4George Müller, *A Narrative of Some of the Lord's Dealings with George Müller* (London: J. Nisbet & Co., 1886).

5George Müller, quoted in Donald Whitney, *Praying the Bible* (Wheaton, IL: Crossway, 2015) 129.

6Jim Elliff, "Introduction to a Million and a Half in Answer to Prayer by George Müller," *Georgemuller.org,* July 8, 2016, http://www.georgemuller.org/devotional/introduction-to-a-million-and-a-half-in-answer-to-prayer-by-george-muller.

7"George Müller: Trusting God for Daily Bread," *Harvestministry.org,* accessed August 1, 2016, http://harvestministry.org/muller.

8George Müller, *Answers to Prayer* (Brookfield, IL: Letcetera Publishing, 2015) 9.

9Corrie ten Boom, "Corrie ten Boom Quote—Prayer," *Christianquotes.info,* accessed August 1, 2016, http://www.christianquotes.info/images/corrie-ten-boom-quote-prayer/.

10"Quote by Oswald Chambers," *Goodreads.com,* accessed August 1, 2016, http://www.goodreads.com/quotes/166479-we-tend-to-use-prayer-as-a-last-resort-but

11"Yada," *Biblehub.com,* accessed August 1, 2016, http://biblehub.com/hebrew/3045.htm.

12Ted Dekker, *Blink of an Eye* (New York: Thomas Nelson, 2007), 280.

Chapter 9: Standing in the Gap

1Charles Bent, "Charles Bent Quotes," *AZquotes.com,* accessed August 1, 2016, http://www.azquotes.com/author/65454-Charles_Bent.

2Philip Sheldrake, ed., *The New Westminster Dictionary of Christian Spirituality* (Louisville, KY: Westminster John Knox Press, 2005), 370.

3J.R.R. Tolkien, *The Return of the King* (New York: Ballantine Books, 1994), 246.

4Oswald Chambers, "Intercessory Prayer," *Utmost.org,* accessed August 1, 2016, http://utmost.org/intercessory-prayer/.

5J.R.R. Tolkien, *The Return of the King* (New York: Ballantine Books, 1994), 919.

6Oswald Chambers, "Intercessory Prayer," *Utmost.org,* accessed August 1, 2016, http://utmost.org/intercessory-prayer/.

7Corrie ten Boom, quoted in Pam Rosewell Moore, *Life Lessons from the Hiding Place: Discovering the Heart of Corrie ten Boom* (Grand Rapids, MI: Chosen Books, 2004), 38.

[8]Leonard Ravenhill, "Leonard Ravenhill Quotes," *AZquotes.com,* accessed August 1, 2016, http://www.azquotes.com/quote/673496.

[9]Alfred Tennyson, "Morte D'Arthur," *Poems* (London: Moxon, 1845), https://library.sc.edu/spcoll/britlit/tenn/morte.html.

[10]C.S. Lewis, *The World's Last Night and Other Essays* (New York: Harcourt, 2002), 8-9.

[11]"Remembering D-Day: The Humanities and the Experience of War," *National Endowment for the Humanities,* June 5, 2014, http://www.neh.gov/divisions/public/featured-project/remembering-d-day-the-humanities-and-the-experience-war.

[12]"World War II: Timeline," *Holocaust Encyclopedia,* accessed August 1, 2016, https://www.ushmm.org/wlc/en/article.php?ModuleId=10007306.

[13]John Eldredge, *Moving Mountains Study Guide: Praying with Passion, Confidence, and Authority* (Nashville, TN: Nelson Books, 2016), 81.

Chapter 10: Disarming Fear

[1]"Florence Nightingale," *Thechristiannetwork.com,* accessed August 1, 2016, http://www.thechristiannetwork.com/florence-nightingale/.

[2]Edwin Hubbell Chapin, quoted in Manford's Magazine, *Volume 37* (Chicago: Tabor, 1893), 587.

[3]"Dunamai," *Biblehub.com,* accessed August 1, 2016, http://biblehub.com/greek/1410.htm.

[4]"Agápē," *Biblehub.com,* accessed August 1, 2016, http://biblehub.com/greek/26.htm.

[5]"Sóphronismos," *Biblehub.com,* accessed August 1, 2016, http://biblehub.com/greek/4995.htm.

[6]"1 Samuel 17:11 Text Analysis," *Biblehub.com,* accessed August 1, 2016, http://biblehub.com/text/1_samuel/17-11.htm.

[7]This quote has been attributed by some sources to Joseph Goebbels; "Joseph Goebbels: The Poison Dwarf," *Holocaust Education and Archives Research Team,* accessed August 1, 2016, http://www.holocaustresearchproject.org/holoprelude/goebbels.html.

[8]"M'Cheyne Quotations," *Mcheyne.info,* accessed August 1, 2016, http://www.mcheyne.info/quotes.php.

[9]Nelson Mandela, "15 of Nelson Mandela's Best Quotes," *USA Today,* December 6, 2013, http://www.usatoday.com/story/news/nation-now/2013/12/05/nelson-mandela-quotes/3775255/.

[10]John Piper, "The Beautiful Faith of Fearless Submission," Sermon, *Bethlehem Baptist Church,* Minneapolis, MN, April 15, 2007, http://www.desiringgod.org/messages/the-beautiful-faith-of-fearless-submission.

[11]John Eldredge, *Wild at Heart: Discovering the Secret of a Man's Soul* (Nashville, TN: Thomas Nelson, 2010), 90.

Chapter 11: Wounds into Weapons

[1]Charles Spurgeon, *Faith's Checkbook: Daily Devotions to Treasure* (Issaquah, WA: Made for Success Publishing, 2014), 14.

[2]"Paraklésis," *Biblehub.com,* accessed August 1, 2016, http://biblehub.com/greek/3874.htm.

[3]Henri Nouwen, *Here and Now: Living in the Spirit* (New York: Crossroad Publishing, 2006), 36.

[4]Nicky Gumbel, "Nicky Gumbel Quotes," *AZquotes.com,* accessed August 1, 2016, http://www.azquotes.com/quote/866168.

[5]Daniel Darling, "How to Build Community in Your Church," *Danieldarling.com,* April 30, 2013, http://www.danieldarling.com/2013/04/how-to-build-community-in-your-church/.

[6]Henri Nouwen, "The Wounded Healer," *Henri Nouwen Society,* accessed August 1, 2016, http://henrinouwen.org/meditation/the-wounded-healer/.

[7]D.T. Niles, quoted in James Simpson, *Simpson's Contemporary Quotations* (Boston, MA: Houghton Mifflin, 1988), 123.

[8]Henri Nouwen, *The Inner Voice of Love: A Journey Through Anguish to Freedom* (New York: Image Books, 1999), 46.

[9]N.T. Wright, *The Challenge of Jesus: Rediscovering Who Jesus Was and Is* (Downer's Grove, IL: InterVarsity, 2015), 184.

Chapter 12: Run

[1]"Skubalon," *Biblehub.com,* accessed August 1, 2016, http://biblehub.com/greek/4657.htm.

[2]Dominique Mosbergen, "This Inspiring Runner Took a Nasty Fall, But She Didn't Stay Down for Long," *Huffington Post,* May 27, 2014, http://www.huffingtonpost.com/2014/05/27/runner-falls-wins-race-heather-dorniden_n_5395232.html.

[3]Ray Vander Laan, *In the Dust of the Rabbi Discovery Guide: 5 Faith Lessons* (Grand Rapids, MI: Zondervan, 2006).

[4]Paul Tripp, *Age of Opportunity* (Phillipsburg, NJ: P&R Publishing, 2001), 115.

[5]Kaj Munk, quoted in Shane Claiborne, *The Irresistible Revolution* (Grand Rapids, MI: Zondervan, 2006), 294.

[6]Carter Conlon, "Run for Your Life," Sermon, *Times Square Church,* New York, NY, September 16, 2001, http://ia600500.us.archive.org/23/items/SERMONINDEX_SID1410/SID1410.mp3.